Editor
Kim Fields

Consultant
Barbara Forslund Cracchiolo, O.T.R.

Editorial Project Manager
Mara Ellen Guckian

Editor-in-Chief
Sharon Coan, M.S. Ed.

Illustrator
Alexandra Artigas

Cover Artist
Brenda DiAntonis

Art Coordinator
Kevin Barnes

Imaging
James Edward Grace
Temo Parra

Product Manager
Phil Garcia

Publishers
Rachelle Cracchiolo, M.S. Ed.
Mary Dupuy Smith, M.S. Ed.

ACTIVITIES FOR
Fine Motor Skills
DEVELOPMENT

Written and Compiled by
Jodene Lynn Smith, M.A.

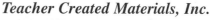

Teacher Created Materials, Inc.
6421 Industry Way
Westminster, CA 92683
www.teachercreated.com

ISBN-0-7439-3689-2

©*2003 Teacher Created Materials, Inc.*

Made in U.S.A.

Table of Contents

Introduction

We have two ways in which we learn things in life. One is through direct learning in which we discover things for ourselves; the other is indirect learning in which we get information from outside ourselves (through television, computers, other people, etc.). When developing fine motor skills, we learn best directly. The term "hands-on learning" is particularly appropriate because this is how we play—with our hands on the toys.

Activities for Fine Motor Skills Development provides ideas for hands-on learning activities in order to develop fine motor skills whereby students can learn about life by discovering things for themselves. Through the use of quick activity descriptions and reproducible pages, teachers will find fun and useful ways to help children learn, practice, and refine their fine motor skills.

The first two sections in this book, "Shoulder and Wrist Activities" and "Wrist and Hand Activities," are sections you may not expect to find in a book about fine motor skills. However, upon further examination, you will discover that strength and stability of the shoulder and wrist directly relate to control of the hand and fingers. These first two sections provide ideas for helping students gain strength in their shoulders, wrists, and hands.

The "Hand and Finger" section is the largest section. It contains ideas for developing what we usually think of as "fine motor control." Although the whole section is devoted to activities which help students develop stability and strength of all the fingers, the emphasis is on activities using the thumb and index finger. We want each student to develop motor control, both fine and gross, as part of the development of a healthy, active child; however, control and coordination of the index finger and thumb are crucial for student success in writing. Finger plays are provided for students to learn poems and songs and their corresponding finger and hand motions. A variety of activities which help students develop control and coordination of their fingers, including activities with pennies and clothespins, are also in this section. Additionally, a large portion of the "Hand and Finger" section is devoted to activities related to using glue, controlling scissors, and writing practice.

Safety Note: Activities described in this book use a variety of materials. Not all materials may be appropriate for the children with whom you are working. For the safety of your students, please consider the children's ages and the size of the materials required when considering whether or not to complete an activity.

What Are Fine Motor Skills?

Fine motor skills refers to the student's ability to use his or her hands to operate tools accurately. Tools commonly used in school include pencils, crayons, scissors, and manipulatives. Precision is not a matter of strength; it is a matter of coordination of the muscles in the hands. We don't expect a three- or four-year-old to hold a pencil correctly to write his or her name. The muscles have not fully developed yet. Large arm and hand movements develop before fine motor skills.

*If pencil skills are pushed too early, students develop poor habits that are difficult to change later on, when they really need to write.

Below are some suggestions for helping students who are having difficulty with their fine motor skills:

- Apply hand lotion to hands.
- Do finger plays.
- Do lacing and stringing activities.
- Eat with a spoon or fork rather than fingers.
- Emphasize easel and chalkboard activities.
- Place small objects in ice cube trays or egg cartons.
- Play with shadow puppets.
- Put money in the piggy bank.
- Roll out play dough.
- Shake dice.
- Use pegs and pegboards.
- Use short pieces of chalk and crayons rather than full-sized ones.
- Use tongs to pick up items.
- Wash hands.

Hand Map

Definitions

> **finger pads**—fingertips
> (See the shaded areas in the illustration.)
>
> **finger opposition**—Thumb touches tip of any finger.
>
> **pincer grasp**—Looks the same as thumb touching index finger except there is a small object between thumb and index finger.
>
> **tripod grasp**—Pencil is held between pads of thumb and index finger and rests on the side of the long finger close to the tip.

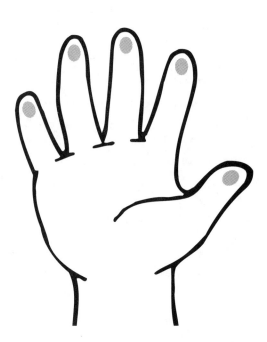

Getting Started

The information on pages 5–8 details areas of development connected to fine motor skills. Suggestions are given for activities to help students with these areas. All students can benefit from participating in these activities.

Motor Planning

Motor planning refers to a student's ability to figure out how to do a new motor task. Some of our motor actions are routine, such as bringing a spoon up to the mouth for eating. If we are asked to bring the spoon to our knee or up to our ear, we would have to think about the movement and plan the motor action. That is motor planning. Prior to any movements, the brain has to organize all the environmental information so that the body will move in the direction needed with the appropriate speed, force, and timing. The ability to motor plan depends on thinking skills as well as sensory motor development.

Below are some suggestions for helping students who are having difficulty with motor planning:

- Break tasks down into smaller steps.

- Do a lot of rolling, jumping, and ball activities.

- Give one direction at a time.

- Guide students through the motor action.

- Have a check-off sheet for each student to check off tasks as he or she completes them.

- Have students orally repeat directions.

- Keep verbal directions to a minimum.

- Minimize verbal and auditory distractions in the room.

- Play imitation games, such as "Simon Says" or "Follow the Leader."

- Play games with movement and rhythm.

- Use visual cues.

Getting Started *(cont.)*

Body Awareness

Body awareness refers to the student's ability to know where his or her body is in space. Opening jar lids without looking at your hands, gauging how far to duck your head when getting under a low table, and sitting down without constantly looking at the chair all require you to have a good sense of where your body is in space.

Other indicators of a student's sense of body awareness include how close or far away he or she sits from other students and how hard or how gently items are pulled apart or put together. Students who have poor body awareness appear clumsy. These students walk by shuffling their feet on the floor, have difficulty climbing on playground equipment, and continually bump into other students.

Heaving, lifting, pushing, pulling, and carrying all help your brain to know where your body is in space. Other suggestions for helping students who are having difficulty with body awareness are listed below. Guide students through the activities until they are comfortable on their own.

- Carry a heavy stack of books.

- Do frog jumps.

- Do jumping activities.

- Do push-ups and pull-ups.

- Play on a jungle gym.

- Play on the monkey bars.

- Play "Simon Says."

- Play tug-of-war.

- Push feet and/or hands against the walls as if to push the walls out.

- Roll on a large exercise ball.

- Start on low playground equipment and then advance to taller equipment.

- Swing by lying on the stomach rather than sitting on the swing seat.

- Take out the garbage.

- Try bean bag activities.

- Use teeter-totters.

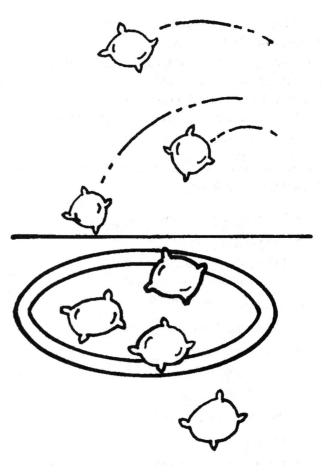

Getting Started *(cont.)*

Bilateral Integration and Crossing Midline

Bilateral integration refers to the student's ability to use both sides of his or her body in an activity. Sometimes our hands are doing the same movement, and at other times they are acting separately. When catching a ball, both hands are doing the same motion. When coloring or writing, one hand is doing the movement while the other hand is holding the paper.

Crossing the midline refers to the student's ability to cross his or her arms or legs over the midline of the body. The midline is an imaginary line that runs through the body, cutting it in half from head to toe. Crossing the midline is the student's ability to reach with the right hand or right leg over the midline to the left side of the body. Crossing the midline means moving an arm or a leg, not moving the body, and twisting toward one side.

Activities that necessitate using both hands, both feet, or crossing over the midline help develop the neuron pathways within the brain for reading, writing, and mathematics. Coordinating both sides of the body is needed for the development of many gross and fine motor skills.

Below are some suggestions for helping students who are having difficulty with bilateral integration or crossing the midline:

- Carry heavy objects with two hands.
- Do jumping jacks.
- Do mixing bowl activities —stir, pour, and measure.
- Jump rope.
- Jump and land with feet apart.
- Play basketball.
- Play clapping games and use rhythm sticks.
- Play musical instruments.
- Play two-square or four-square.
- Practice cutting.
- Practice opening snack and lunch containers.
- Ride a bike.

- Roll clay.
- Scissor-walk on a line.
- Sharpen pencils using a manual pencil sharpener.
- Skip.
- String beads.
- Swim.
- Tear paper.
- Tie shoes, or tie yarn bows on packages.
- Turn a hand eggbeater.
- Use pop beads or interlocking blocks.
- Wind wind-up toys.

Getting Started *(cont.)*

Tactile Awareness

Tactile awareness refers to the student's sense of touch. Skin is the largest sensory area on our bodies. The palms of our hands and the bottoms of our feet are the most sensitive. Students who are tactile defensive, or overly sensitive to touch, will be reluctant to touch many materials such as play dough, glue, finger paint, or other messy items. These students may be very selective of what foods and textures they eat. We are constantly using our sense of touch for everything we do. Tactile receptors are located under the skin all over our bodies. Receptors in our hands help us to know whether an object is soft, hard, hot, cold, bumpy, smooth, etc. Tactile receptors also let us know when a breeze blows across our arms or legs. Tactile receptors in our mouths let us know if we have food in our mouths.

Below are some suggestions for helping students who are having difficulty with tactile awareness:

- Allow a tactile defensive student to go first or last in line so other students don't rub against him or her.

- Avoid approaching the student from the back; always let him or her see you approaching.

- Avoid unexpected touching of the student.

- Don't force, but encourage, participation in tactile activities.

- Encourage gradual exposure to messy experiences, even if only momentary.

- Encourage hand washing.

- Encourage student to pull and push heavy objects.

- Let student have his or her own personal space, such as a carpet square when sitting on the floor.

- Let student initiate touch.

- Let student rub various textures on his or her arms and legs.

- Offer a variety of manipulatives.

- Provide a variety of sensory experiences such as a bean table, water table, or sand table.

- Provide an escape, such as a quiet corner away from too much sensation.

- Use a firm touch on student's arms, legs, and back rather than a light touch.

Early Childhood Development

The accompanying developmental checklists suggest fine motor skills for children eighteen months through five years of age. The skills are arranged in groupings of several months at a time and are meant to be used as a guide rather than as a rigid timetable. This information will help you to anticipate stages of normal child development in the area of fine motor skills. Each child will acquire these skills at his or her own pace. Some children develop them more quickly in one area and more slowly in another. Consider creating a file folder for each child in which to keep checklists, records, and anecdotal notes.

The toddler stage (eighteen months to three years old) is an exciting period of growth for children. They explore their environment using all five senses. They are the center of their universe, and the world revolves around them.

As children near the age of two, the experience does not have to become one of uncontrollable terror and mayhem. At this time, children are beginning to explore how much they can control their universe and what the limits are. The words "no" and "yes" become powerful ones, allowing them to take ownership of their own boundaries. With gentle guidance from parents and teachers, children can form limits of control that are compatible with the needs of others as well as their own.

Learning for a toddler often occurs when an activity can be repeated over and over. For example, a toddler loves to dump things out or over, put them back, and then do it again repeatedly. This simple activity is a challenge, and the child is striving to master it. There is delight in every accomplishment.

The preschooler is becoming more autonomous. As he or she improves fine motor skills, the child is able to meet many needs with little help from an adult. Dressing, undressing, using the bathroom, and eating are some activities a preschooler can now do independently from an adult.

Preschoolers spend most of their time playing. Play is very important to their development. Play offers an excellent opportunity for language development. They enjoy playing in groups of peers, participating in dramatic play, and having a chance to stretch their imaginations.

A series of Fine Motor Skills Checklists can be found on pages 10 –13. Of course, these are only guidelines. Every child has an individual pace and should not be compared to other children in general. Comparisons only become useful when a child's abilities are extremely disparate from others of his or her own age. Further investigation into the cause of such variances may be worthwhile. Be aware of differences, but do not jump to conclusions. Most likely, any variance is within normal range.

Fine Motor Skills Checklist

Child: _____ **Date(s):** _____

Check all mastered fine motor skills.

- ❑ builds a four-piece cube tower

- ❑ clasps hands

- ❑ completes a three-piece form board (circle, square, triangle)

- ❑ folds paper

- ❑ imitates crayon stroke

- ❑ inverts container spontaneously to obtain an object

- ❑ makes horizontal, vertical, and circular scribble after demonstration

- ❑ places six large round pegs into pegboard without help

- ❑ pounds, squeezes, or pulls off bits of clay

- ❑ puts four rings on a peg

- ❑ rolls a ball in imitation

- ❑ scoops with spoon or shovel

- ❑ strings one 1" (2.5 cm) bead

- ❑ throws a small ball

Fine Motor Skills Checklist

Child: _____ **Date(s):** _____

Check all mastered fine motor skills.

- ❑ aligns three cubes to make a train
- ❑ builds a tower with six to eight cubes
- ❑ completes a three- to five-piece puzzle
- ❑ cuts 5" (13 cm) paper in half
- ❑ draws circles, imitating an adult
- ❑ draws horizontal and vertical lines, imitating an adult
- ❑ folds paper in half in imitation
- ❑ hands work together in opposing motion
- ❑ hands work together in similar motion
- ❑ holds a pencil or crayon with thumb and fingers
- ❑ holds scissors correctly
- ❑ imitates three-block bridge, using cubes
- ❑ makes first spontaneous designs
- ❑ manipulates hands and fingers in finger paint
- ❑ manipulates, pounds, and squeezes clay
- ❑ nests objects graduated in size
- ❑ places tiny objects in small container
- ❑ points with his or her index finger
- ❑ pounds pegs into a work bench
- ❑ rolls clay balls
- ❑ scribbles with a circular motion
- ❑ snips with scissors, begins to cut 5" (13 cm) paper in half
- ❑ strings five to ten ½" (1.3 cm) beads
- ❑ takes apart and puts together snap toys
- ❑ touches index finger with thumb
- ❑ turns knobs
- ❑ unscrews a jar lid
- ❑ unwraps objects wrapped in paper (e.g., candy)

Fine Motor Skills Checklist

Preschoolers: 36 months to 48 months

Child: _____ Date(s): _____

Check all mastered fine motor skills.

❑ begins to show hand preference

❑ cuts dough or soft clay with a cookie cutter

❑ cuts 5" (13 cm) paper in two

❑ folds paper in half without a model

❑ grasps pencil between thumb and forefinger (tripod grasp)

❑ imitates drawing a cross

❑ imitates drawing a diagonal line

❑ makes first designs or spontaneous forms

❑ places six pegs in a pegboard

❑ puts tiny objects in a small container

❑ puts together a six- to eight-piece puzzle

❑ strings beads

❑ unscrews and screws a 3" (8 cm) lid

❑ winds up a wind-up toy

Fine Motor Skills Checklist

Child: _____ Date(s): _____

Check all mastered fine motor skills.

- ❑ builds a five-block bridge through imitation
- ❑ builds structures with blocks or connecting toys
- ❑ completes inset puzzles with five to ten pieces
- ❑ creases paper with fingers
- ❑ cuts a triangle with 2" (5 cm) sides within ½" (1.3 cm) accuracy
- ❑ cuts 5" (13 cm) square within ½" (1.3 cm) accuracy
- ❑ cuts pictures from a magazine
- ❑ draws a line from one object to another
- ❑ draws a person with a head and three clear features, such as arms and legs
- ❑ draws a square, imitating an adult
- ❑ draws a recognizable picture
- ❑ places key in lock and opens lock
- ❑ places small pegs in holes on a board
- ❑ prints own first name with a model
- ❑ puts paper clip on paper
- ❑ strings small beads, reproducing color and shape sequence
- ❑ traces letters
- ❑ usually uses dominant hand
- ❑ writes a few identifiable letters/numerals and attempts first name

Starter Activities

To gain fine motor strength and coordination students will have to use their hands and especially their fingers in order to do activities. A good awareness of the sense of touch is an excellent place to begin when thinking about motor control activities. Helping students feel comfortable in using their sense of touch will aid in their ability and willingness to do many of the other activities in this book. The activities on this page and the next develop children's kinesthetic awareness, and refine their sense of touch. These, and similar activities, are good precursors to the fine motor activities explored in this book.

Texture Hunt

Review the various ways an object can feel—bumpy, smooth, rough, soft, or hard. Have students walk around the room touching a variety of objects. Challenge them to find one object that feels like each texture described.

Provide a variety of textures for students to touch. Be sure to include objects such as sandpaper, wax paper, bubble wrap, a rock, pudding, oil, carpet, tile, wallpaper samples, brushes, tinfoil, etc.

Button Grab

Collect a variety of buttons and place them in a bag or box that students cannot see through. Have each student close his or her eyes and select two buttons out of the bag, placing one button in each hand. Have the child describe the shape of the button by using the sense of touch. Can the student tell which button is larger by touch alone?

Banana Dig

Make a box of pudding according to the package directions. Put pudding in a small cup for each child. Slice the bananas and "hide" the slices in the pudding. Have students reach into the pudding in order to pull the bananas out and eat them. Begin by allowing students to have their eyes open. Then, have students close their eyes and find the bananas without looking. **Teacher Note:** Handwashing prior to this activity is a must!

Starter Activities *(cont.)*

Mystery Bag

Place a variety of items in a bag that students cannot see through. (Be sure your students know the name of each item.) Have your students reach in the bag and try to identify the objects. Then, name an object and see if the students can pull that object out of the bag.

Letter Writing

Pair students. Have the children write on each other's backs using their index fingers. Students can draw shapes or write letters, numbers, or words on each other's backs. Challenge the student whose back is being written on to figure out what has been written. Then have the children change places.

Rubbing Lotion

Let students rub various textures on their arms and legs. Lotion is a good substance to use because it is absorbed; however, if you would like to get messy, students can rub pudding, paint, ketchup, glue, cooking oil, and anything else you can think of that will not harm their skin. Have students rub soap over their arms and hands while cleaning up.

Art Activities

Activities that strengthen the shoulder and wrist help students with stability and control when writing or doing fine motor activities. When you look at infants, they use gross motor movements such as swatting at a object rather than using the thumb and fingers in order to pick up an object. The same is true for motor skills appropriate for toddlers and young children. Children need to develop good shoulder and wrist control before they gain refinement of hand skills and refined fine motor coordination. Strengthening the larger shoulder and wrist muscles first will ease the development of smaller muscles in the hand.

Vertical and Horizontal Art

Painting, writing, and drawing on an easel or paper-covered wall allows for a greater range of motion for a child than an 8 ½" x 11" (22 cm x 28 cm) sheet of paper.

Alter the surfaces that students write, draw, or paint on to help them develop shoulder and wrist stability. Have each student try the following:

- While standing, draw on paper attached to the wall.
- While kneeling, draw on paper attached to the wall.
- While lying on his or her stomach, draw on paper.
- While outdoors, use a paintbrush or roller to paint with water on concrete or on a wall.

Branch Painting

Use some of the following activities to help develop stability in students' shoulders and wrists. You will want to do this activity outside. Hang a large piece of butcher paper on the wall low enough for students to reach, yet high enough so that students will have to use their shoulders to reach to the upper portions of the paper. Collect a variety of sizes of leafy branches (pepper tree branches work well). Fill a small tub, or roasting pan, with watered-down paint. Students lay the branches in the paint and then use the branches to paint on the piece of butcher paper. The motion used is more of an "overhead" swatting motion than applying brush strokes.

Note: Be sure that students are spaced far apart and that this activity is well supervised.

Marble Activities

Marble Painting

Place a sheet of white construction paper in the basin of a plastic tub. Spoon in a small amount (about the size of a quarter) of watered-down paint onto the paper. Place a marble inside the tub. To create a picture, each student must hold the tub with both of his or her hands and roll the marble around inside the tub. The result is a beautiful and unique art project. You may choose to add two or three colors of paint; however, limit the total amount of paint so that the paper does not become too wet.

Marble Roll

Locate a container (such as a washing tub) that students can easily hold in their hands. Randomly place stickers with the numbers 1–5 in the basin of the tub. Place a marble (a washer or magnet will work) inside the tub. Have each student hold the tub in his or her hands and roll the marble around the basin of the tub to each of the stickers in the correct order. You may choose to use letters printed on the stickers or small stickers with a variety of characters on them. Then, you can call out the type of sticker that you want students to roll the marble on.

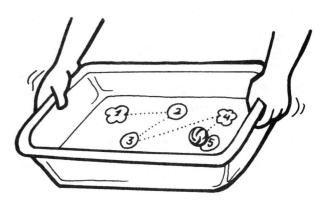

Roll to the Hole

Use a box and a golf ball for this activity. Cut out a hole or holes in the bottom of the box. Make the hole(s) a little larger than the golf ball. The student places the ball in the box and, holding either side of the box, tilts the box from side-to-side, trying to get the ball to drop through the hole. This activity can be done sitting on the floor or standing. If done standing, have the child stand over carpet, sand, or grass. Otherwise the ball will go rolling!

Safety Note: Use golf balls or other small, heavy balls if marbles are too small for your students.

Pretending Activities

Sweeping

Have each student hold onto a broom with both hands on the handle with the bristles resting on the floor. The student should sweep by bringing the broom handle across, in front of the body. The bristles should continue to touch the floor. He or she practices sweeping a ball (or a crumpled-up newspaper ball) back and forth along the floor. Encourage the students not to push the ball too hard; they should be able to reach it again without moving their feet. When students are confident, set up an obstacle course to sweep a ball through. Have students use a push broom to use a different range of motion.

Streamers

Try some creative movement with students. Give each student two 2'–3' (61–91 cm) paper streamers, one for each hand. Set the movement to music (classical music often works well). Encourage the students to spread out in the movement area. Have each student fully extend his or her arms while holding the streamers. Give some of the following commands for the student to demonstrate with his or her streamers:

- Be a snowflake fluttering slowly down, twirling around.
- Be a bolt of lightning shooting down.
- Be the wind blowing all about.
- Be a butterfly flying through the air.
- Be a bumblebee looking for a flower.

Hammering Nails

Purchase Styrofoam (at a local craft store) in blocks that are at least 3" (8 cm) thick. You don't have to purchase Styrofoam; it comes in mail-order packages, as well as in boxes that protect large items such as TVs, computers, radios, etc.

Provide at least 20 golf tees, a wooden mallet, and a piece of Styrofoam for each student. Have the student hold the "nail" (the golf tee) carefully and gently tap it with the wooden mallet until it is embedded in the Styrofoam. As students become used to tapping the golf tees into the Styrofoam, encourage them to create designs or patterns.

Teacher Note: A real hammer, nails, and wood may be used if working in a small group situation where students can be closely monitored.

Games

Spoon Walk

Give each child a wooden spoon with a long handle. Have the child practice walking around while carrying an object inside the bowl of the spoon. Begin with stable objects such as beanbags. As the student's skills improve, change the object to a small ball or marble. If carrying the spoon by the handle is difficult for students, have them grasp the handle closer to the bowl of the spoon. As stability increases, have students move their hands back farther on the handle.

This activity can be turned into a relay. Provide a bowl of 20 marbles, an empty bowl, and a wooden spoon for each team. Place the empty bowl at the opposite end of the room. The first student from each team places a marble on the spoon and walks to the other side of the room and drops the marble into the empty bowl. The student then returns the spoon to the next person in line, who then repeats the action. Two teams compete with one another to see which team can move all of the marbles to the other bowl first.

Pantomime

Children are usually very excited when they are first introduced to pantomime. Pantomime allows for creativity, and if the activities are selected carefully, pantomime helps develop shoulder strength and control. Choose one student to be the actor. The remaining students can guess what activity is being acted out. Once the action has been correctly guessed, give all of the children a chance to act out an activity.

Have students pretend to:

- shoot an arrow
- chop down a tree with an ax
- put on an apron
- build a building with blocks
- put on a coat
- put on gloves

- wrap a gift
- play the guitar
- hammer a nail into the wall and hang a picture
- scoop ice cream
- put a key in a treasure chest and open it

- climb up and down a ladder
- hang laundry on a clothesline
- paddle downstream
- put on overalls
- dig a big hole with a shovel

Games *(cont.)*

Going Fishing

Create fishing poles by cutting ½" (1.3 cm) dowel rods into sections about 2' (61 cm) long. Staple a piece of string that is about 2' (61 cm) long to one of the ends of the dowel. Tie a doughnut-hole magnet at the other end of the string. Create a pond by shaping a piece of blue yarn into a circle on the floor. A large piece of blue fabric or a sheet could also be used as the pond. Make a fishing game by marking the fish patterns (pages 103 and 164) according to some of the ideas listed below. (You may wish to laminate the fish for durability.) Hook a paper clip on each fish; then place the fish in the pond. A student catches the fish on his or her pole. (The magnet attracts the paper clip.) Then he or she works in a small group to match the fish in one of the following ways:

Sequencing numbers—Students arrange numbers written on the fish in sequential order.

Counting match—Write numbers on some fish and a corresponding number of dots on other fish. Students match each fish with dots on it to the fish with the corresponding number.

Color words—Students match same-colored fish.

Compound words—Write one word on each fish. Students match two words that can be placed together to form a compound word. Or use blends, and have students make words. (c–at, d–og, sp–ot, bl–ow)

Contractions—Write a contraction on one fish and the words that make up the contraction on two other fish. A student matches a contraction to the two words that make up the contraction.

Sight words—Students catch a sight word; then try to read it.

O's on a Bumpy Road

Draw a wavy line on the blackboard. Have each student stand on a sheet of construction paper facing the chalkboard, in the middle of the line. The student remains on the paper while completing this activity. Starting at the left side of the line, he or she draws O's on top of the line, then continues until the end of the line is reached. When the student has finished, have him or her draw O's under the line. Challenge the student to draw as many O's as possible.

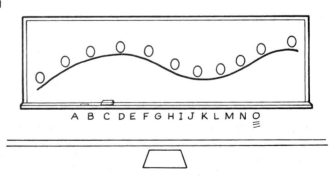

Spreading Activities

Have students practice spreading different materials with a knife. Spread ketchup, mustard, pudding, thick paint, toothpaste, finger paint, shaving cream, or hair gel. Try spreading materials on: bread, tortillas, cake, sturdy crackers, cardboard, or paper. Try some of the following activities in order to make food to eat or just to practice the spreading motion in order to strengthen the wrist. (**Safety Note:** Always check for food allergies prior to the activity.)

Activities that strengthen the wrist and hand help students with stability (control) when performing fine motor activities. Everyday activities such as twisting, spreading, and scooping help strengthen the intrinsic muscles in the hand and help to develop in-hand manipulation and coordination between the thumb and fingers that are necessary to develop the refinement of fine motor skills. Use the activities here and on pages 22–54 to help develop stability in students' wrists and hands.

Peanut Butter

Have students spread peanut butter on crackers. Make your own peanut butter. Place 1 cup (240 mL) roasted shelled peanuts and 1 teaspoon (5 mL) oil in a blender and close the top. Blend several minutes. Use a rubber spatula to scrape the mixture from the blender. Blend until it is easy to spread. Spread the peanut butter on crackers. Serve with a drink.

Ants on a Log

To make Ants on a Log, clean celery and cut it into 3" (8 cm) sections. Have children spread peanut butter or cream cheese inside the celery and place raisins on top.

Sandwiches

Provide plastic knives, bread, peanut butter, and jelly for each student to make a peanut butter and jelly sandwich. Have students wash their hands before participating in this activity. Older students can scoop the peanut butter and jelly out of the jars. An adult can do the scooping for younger students. Have students spread the peanut butter and jelly onto the bread. When the ingredients are on the bread, have each student fold the sandwich in half and eat it.

Twisting Activities

Container Lids

Collect a variety of containers with lids. Take off the lids and place them in one pile. Place the containers in a separate pile. A student finds the matching lid for each container and replaces it. **Variation:** Collect some containers that have lids that snap on, and some that twist on.

Wind-up Toys

Collect a variety of wind-up toys for students to play with. A child winds the key, using his or her thumb and fingers, in order to make the toy move.

Lid Rotation

Provide a lid from a peanut butter jar, a 2-liter soda bottle, or a baby food jar for students to practice rotating. Begin with the lid on the table. A student places his or her fingertips and thumb in a tripod grasp in order to hold onto the perimeter of the lid. Have the student rotate the lid by taking it off the table, rotating the lid with his or her fingers, and then placing the lid back on the table. He or she picks the lid back up off the table, rotates it, and then sets it back down on the table again. The child continues until the lid has been turned 360 degrees. You may want to make a mark on the lid with a permanent marker so that the student will have a beginning and ending point. Then, have the student pick up the lid and rotate it 360 degrees before putting it down again. Have the student rotate the lid to the left, then to the right. Add water or beans to the lid in order to make it heavier. Begin with the lid of a baby food jar. Then, as students become skilled at rotating a baby food jar lid, try a smaller lid such as the lid to a 2-liter bottle of soda.

Squeezing Activities

Tube Squeeze

Have students practice using their hands to squeeze tubes of toothpaste, ketchup, icing, and hair gel. Fill empty plastic bottles (ketchup, mustard, etc.) with water. Allow children to water plants or a lawn by squeezing the water out of the containers.

Glue Art

Give each child an 8½" x 11" (22 cm x 28 cm) sheet of white paper. Have each student squeeze a bottle of glue in a random design on top of the paper; then allow the glue to dry thoroughly. Once dry, have him or her use either watercolor paints or a mixture of half tempera paint and half water to whitewash over the glue design. For an added challenge, have the student create the outline of an object when squeezing the glue. This requires excellent hand and wrist control.

One-Drop Circles

Take an eyedropper and fill it with water. (Add some food coloring to the water if desired.) Draw a series of circles or balloons on a sheet of paper for each student. Have him or her squeeze just one drop of water into each circle, not a whole eyedropper full. Once he or she has practiced and gained good control over the eyedropper, have him or her create a picture on white construction paper with this technique.

Lemonade

Provide a collection of lemons that have already been sliced in half. Have each student take turns squeezing the lemons into a cup or container in order to make lemonade. Strain the seeds from the juice. Add some sugar and water and allow the students to drink what they have made.

Teacher Note: Direct students to squeeze the lemons with the cut-side up to prevent seeds from dropping in the lemonade. Always remember to wash hands first.

Squeezing Activities *(cont.)*

Spray Bottles

Fill a spray bottle with water. (Use a squirt gun if you want to focus on index finger control.) Have each student practice spraying the water out of the bottle. Draw a circle, or another shape, on the ground with a piece of chalk. The student squirts water out of the bottle into the shape. Instruct him or her to get the whole shape wet. In addition, students can use the water to make shapes, letters, or numbers.

Add food coloring to the water in the spray bottle. Provide each student with a rag to place on the ground. A student sprays the rag, trying to get it entirely wet. The student can see very easily where he or she has sprayed the rag because it will be colored.

Bag of Paint

Fill resealable, plastic bags with poster paint and a little bit of cornstarch (to thicken). Cut a small corner off each bag. Allow each student to create a picture by squeezing the paint out of the bag onto a sheet of paper.

Sponge Squeeze

Provide a bucket of water and sponges. Have each student squeeze water out of sponges using both hands. As a student becomes skilled with both hands, have him or her isolate one hand, then the other.

This activity can be turned into a relay race, too. Provide a bucket of water and a sponge for each relay team. Place an empty cup or bucket for each relay team 10' (3 m) from the bucket of water. Soak the sponge by placing it in the water bucket. A student picks up the water-soaked sponge and runs to the empty cup. There, he or she squeezes as much water as possible into the empty cup, and returns the sponge to the water bucket for the next teammate to use. The team that fills the empty cup first wins.

Squeezing Activities *(cont.)*

Hole Punch

Have students punch holes in a paper plate using a hole punch. As students become skilled at using the hole punch, have them punch holes around the outside edge of shapes traced on tagboard. Then, students can use those shapes as lacing cards. (See pages 101–103 for shapes appropriate for lacing cards.)

Stapled Tambourine

Allow students to practice squeezing by using a stapler. (Be sure to discuss stapler safety before giving a stapler to a young child.) A fun way to practice stapling is to make a tambourine out of two paper plates. A child faces the inside (top) of two paper plates toward each other. He or she then staples the edges of the paper plates. Just before the paper plates are completely stapled closed, the child puts a handful of beans inside, then continues stapling the paper plates closed. Have each student practice using his or her tambourine while you play music on the radio.

Squeezing Utensils

Use chopsticks, salad tongs, tweezers, or clothespins for students to practice the squeezing motion, as well as the open/close motion. Begin by simply having students practice picking up objects, such as cotton balls, beans, buttons, jacks, etc.

Then, have students practice moving the objects from one location to another. For example, students can move cotton balls from the table into a bowl, or from the table into a trash can on the other side of the room.

As a student becomes skilled at moving an object from one place to another, have him or her use an ice cube tray or egg carton to practice moving the objects. Place one cotton ball (or other object) in one compartment of the egg carton. Have each student use tweezers or another utensil to pick up the object and move it to the next compartment. Direct him or her to move the object from compartment to compartment, until the object has been in each compartment. For a special treat, use a piece of candy. Once the object has been in each compartment, the student may eat the piece of candy.

Shaking Activities

Wave Machine

Fill an empty 16 oz. (480 mL) clear plastic water bottle about half full with mineral oil. Then, add water to make the bottle three quarters full. Add a drop of blue food coloring. Make sure that you put the top back on firmly. It helps to secure the top onto the bottle, so that students cannot undo it accidentally. Have students hold the bottle on its side and slowly rock it back and forth to watch the waves, using one or both hands.

Shaking Dice

Students can practice shaking dice in their hands; however, it is always more fun if there is a game to accompany this action. Older students may enjoy playing board games. Younger students may enjoy shaking and releasing the dice 10 times and tallying how many times each number appears.

Food Shake

Place the ingredients for instant pudding in an empty jar, being sure to seal the lid tightly. Have each student take a turn shaking the jar to make the pudding. Or place heavy cream in an empty jar, being sure to seal the lid tightly. Have each student take a turn shaking the jar to make the butter.

Tube of Beans

Fill a tennis-ball tube with beans and replace the cap. Have a student shake the tube by rotating his or her wrists back and forth in order to make the sounds. Then, have him or her shake the tube twice with the right hand, and then twice with the left hand. He or she continues with a variety of patterns, alternating between right and left hands.

Flipping Activities

Provide a spatula and a variety of objects for students to practice the flipping motion. Students can scoop up bean bags, wadded-up paper, paper plates, play food such as pancakes, eggs, etc. Have each student practice flipping the item upside down. Then, the student can practice using the spatula to flip objects behind his or her back.

Once a student becomes skilled at being able to flip an object upside down and into the air, challenge him or her to flip an object in the air with a spatula and then catch it again on the spatula. This will take wrist control for the student to do the flipping motion, and hand-eye coordination for him or her to catch the object.

Flip It In

Provide an empty box, such as a shoe box, and challenge students to flip objects into it. Move the box farther away in order to make the activity more difficult.

Beanbag Flip

Enlarge the pattern of an animal onto tagboard in order to make a beanbag board. (Most of the animal patterns in this book will work.) Cut holes where appropriate. Have each student use his or her hands or a spatula to try to flip a beanbag into the nose or eyes of the animal. You can keep score of this game if desired. Allocate a point value for the eyes and the nose and have students play until they reach a predetermined number of points.

Juggling Scarves

Provide each child with two different colored scarves. Scarves can be made out of 12" (30 cm) squares of fabric. Teach each child how to hold the scarf in the center, extend his/her arm over his/her head and flip the scarf into the air. Then, the student catches the scarf at waist level. Give verbal cues (call out a color) for which scarf is to be flipped in the air and caught. Call out colors in a rhythmic timing. See who can "juggle" the scarves the longest.

Scooping Activities

Provide a large spoon for students to practice scooping objects. The following objects work well for scooping activities: cotton balls, beans, pasta, crayons, paper clips, magnetic letters, etc. Try the following scooping activities:

Floor Scoop

Place objects in a bowl and have each student scoop the objects out of the bowl and onto the table or floor. Then, have him or her scoop the objects from the table or floor back into the bowl.

Bowl Scoop

Place objects in one bowl and have each student scoop the objects from one bowl to the other bowl.

Scoop, Walk, and Drop

Place objects in a bowl. Place an empty bowl on the other side of the room. Have each student scoop objects (one at a time) out of the bowl, walk across the room, and drop the objects into the empty bowl.

Find and Scoop

Place objects in a container of rice. Require each student to use a slotted spoon in order to scoop the objects out of the rice.

Pouring Activities

Practice pouring activities by having students pour the following: lemonade, water, rice, beans, salt, and sand.

Larger to Smaller to Larger

Provide a scoop (or spoon), small plastic or paper cups, a container of rice, and a larger container for students to experiment with scooping and pouring. Have each student scoop rice from the rice container into smaller cups. Once all of the smaller cups are full, have him or her pick up the smaller cups and pour each of the cups of rice into a larger container or back into the original rice container.

Liquid Measurement

Gather a pitcher and containers measuring a cup, pint, quart, and gallon. First, children should take a pitcher to the sink and fill it with water. Next, they fill and experiment with the containers provided. Young children can experiment by simply pouring water from container to container. Challenge older children to find the answers to the questions on page 30.

Use household items that are the appropriate size for the containers. It works best to provide plastic containers that are clear, so the student can see if the container is full. If the containers being used at this center are not already marked, label each with the appropriate word: cup, pint, quart, or gallon.

Funnel Pouring with Sand

Have a child place a funnel securely in the top of a cup. Next, have him or her scoop up some dry sand in another cup and slowly pour it into the funnel. After the cup of sand has been poured through the funnel, have him or her remove the funnel and place it on the now empty cup. Using the cup of sand, the child pours the sand through the funnel into the other cup. Encourage each child to repeat this activity, pouring back and forth from cup to cup several times.

By using cups or pitchers of different shapes and sizes, children will begin to grasp the concept that the same amount of a substance looks like a different amount in a different-sized container.

For a fun art project, use a funnel to layer different colors of sand in a container (a baby food jar works well). Secure the jars with lids and allow the students to take them home.

Pouring Activities *(cont.)*

Directions: Experiment with the measuring cups and water. Try to answer each of the questions.

Liquid Measurement Chart
1. Find the cup. Use it to fill the pint. How many cups in a pint?   _____   c   =   p
2. Find the pint. Use it to fill the quart. How many pints in a quart?   _____   p   =   qt
3. Find the quart. Use it to fill the gallon. How many quarts in a gallon?   _____   qt   =   G
4. Find the cup. Use it to fill the quart. How many cups in a quart?   _____   c   =   qt
5. Find the pint. Use it to fill the gallon. How many pints in a gallon?   _____   p   =   G
6. Find the cup. Use it to fill the gallon. How many cups in a gallon?   _____   c   =   G

Teacher Note: If desired, use the following substitutions: cup (240 mL), pint (475 mL), quart (950 mL), and gallon (240 mL).

Art Activities

Wind-Up Yarn

Have each student wrap yarn around an empty paper-towel roll. He or she holds the roll with one hand and winds the yarn around the roll with the other hand. The student keeps rolling until all the yarn is wound up. Have the student wind the yarn around a pencil for a fine motor skill challenge.

Toothbrush Art

Provide each student with a toothbrush. Remind the student not to place the toothbrush in his or her mouth. The student pretends to brush his or her teeth, keeping the toothbrush on the outside of the mouth. Then, the student may dip the toothbrush in paint and use it to paint letters on a sheet of paper.

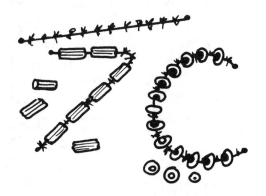

Shapes

Have each student string cereal, drinking-straw pieces, pasta, or beads onto pipe cleaners. Then, the student may form the pipe cleaners into shapes, letters, and numbers.

Diamonds

Create this unique art project by crossing two very small dowel rods in a + shape for each child. Tie the intersection with a pipe cleaner. Have the child weave multicolored yarn around the dowels to form a colorful diamond. Begin at the star.

   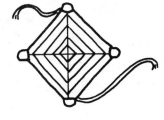

Stamping Activities

Gather together paper, ink pads, and a variety of stamps. Allow students to experiment with the stamps to create a picture. If the images on the stamps are large enough, have the students color the pictures when they are finished. This activity can be turned into a skills exercise by having students use the stamps to illustrate concepts being taught in class. For example, each student can use the stamps to create a picture, then write a number sentence to go with it.

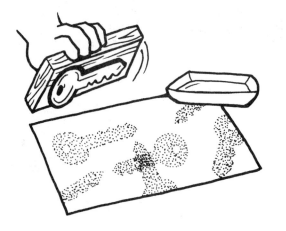

Key Stamps

Ahead of time, use a hot glue gun to glue keys to small pieces of wood. Provide each child with a variety of key stamps, paper, and ink pads. Allow him or her to make key pictures by stamping the wood block into the ink and then onto the paper.

Burlap Block Stamps

Glue burlap to the bottom of wooden blocks. (Scrap wood in a variety of shapes works well on this project.) Provide paint and paper for each child to use. A child dips burlap blocks into paint and presses them onto paper. He or she can form letters or make pictures.

Car Track Stamps

Provide students with paper, paint, and a variety of toy cars. Encourage each child to dip a car in the paint; then drive the car all over his or her paper. For added artistic effect, allow each child to use more than one car and color of paint.

Printing Activities

Marshmallow Prints

Marshmallows can be used as circle stamps. A child dips a marshmallow in paint and then presses it onto paper to create a colorful picture. (Allow him or her to use several different marshmallows.) He or she may use the marshmallow as a stamp to create circle patterns on the paper, or drag the marshmallow along the paper as a sort of paintbrush. Allow each student to experiment to see which way he or she prefers to stamp.

Apple Prints

Cut apples into halves ahead of time. Or, if desired, let the children use plastic knives to quarter the apples. Using a large sheet of white drawing paper and crayons, have each child draw and color the trunk and branches of a tree. To add leaves to the tree, the child selects half an apple and red, yellow, or green paint. He or she presses the apple in the paint, blots it on a paper towel, and presses the apple onto the colored tree. If desired, children can use the apples to make prints in different colors or use their apples to make prints on the Apple Print Tree (see page 34).

Potato Prints

Ahead of time, cut a potato in half. Using a pen, trace a shape, such as a heart or star on the flat, cut surface. Carve around the shape until it stands out from the potato. (You may wish to prepare several different potato stamps.) Pour poster paint into a pie plate or other container so that it is easy to dip the potato into the paint without spills. For each child, provide a sheet of 8½" x 5" (22 cm x 13 cm) paper that is folded in half like a card. A child dips the potato stamp into the paint, then onto the paper. The child can decorate the paper to make a card for a special occasion. Consider using cookie cutters as an alternative to potato stamps.

Printing Activities (cont.)

Apple Print Tree

Directions: Use apple pieces dipped in paint to make apple prints on the tree.

Pretending Activities

Dress Up

Provide each student with a doll or stuffed animal with clothes that fit. Have the student practice dressing the doll or animal. You may also provide dress-up clothes for the students to try on themselves. Be sure to include clothes that have a variety of closings including: buttons, zippers, Velcro®, clasps, and laces.

Tying Knots

Create a clothesline by tying a string to two chairs and pulling the chairs apart so that they form a taut line. Provide fabric strips and have each student attach the fabric strips to the clothesline by tying a simple knot or bow.

Turn Around

Provide each student with a pair of socks. Have him or her turn each sock inside-out. After both socks are inside-out, have the student turn the socks rightside-in. This activity can be done with other items of clothing as well. Have each student turn the jacket that he or she is wearing inside-out and then rightside-in again.

Car Wash

Provide students with a bucket of water and sponges. Have them wash small cars and trucks with the sponges. Students can practice a larger motor skill by washing tricycles and bicycles with the sponge. If desired, add a small amount of mild soap to the water.

Explorations

Float or Sink?

Collect a variety of objects and display them on a tray. Fill a container with water. A child takes one item at a time from the tray, and guesses if the object will float or sink. Then, he or she drops the item into the water tub and decides if the correct conclusion was made about the item. The child follows the same procedure for all objects on the tray. Younger children can experiment with the objects. Older children can complete the worksheet on page 37.

Magnets

Provide different-sized magnets and a tray with a variety of objects on it. (Make sure to include some objects that will attract a magnet.) Using any of the magnets provided, a child finds out which objects on the tray are attracted to the magnet by using the magnet to try to attract the objects. Have him or her sort the objects into two groups, one for the objects attracted to the magnet, and another for the objects not attracted. Younger children can experiment with the magnet. Older children can complete the worksheet on page 38.

Magnetic Letters

Provide students with a container of magnetic letters and a magnetic surface (a cookie sheet works well). Allow each student to manipulate the letters and stick them to the magnetic surface. Younger students can try to identify letters. Older students can use the letters to create words. If students do not know how to spell any words, provide index cards labeled with simple words. Students can search for the correct letters to spell words.

Explorations *(cont.)*

Float or Sink?

Directions: Circle the items that float. Put an X on the items that sink.

Explorations (cont.)

Magnets

Directions: Put a circle around each object that a magnet attracts.

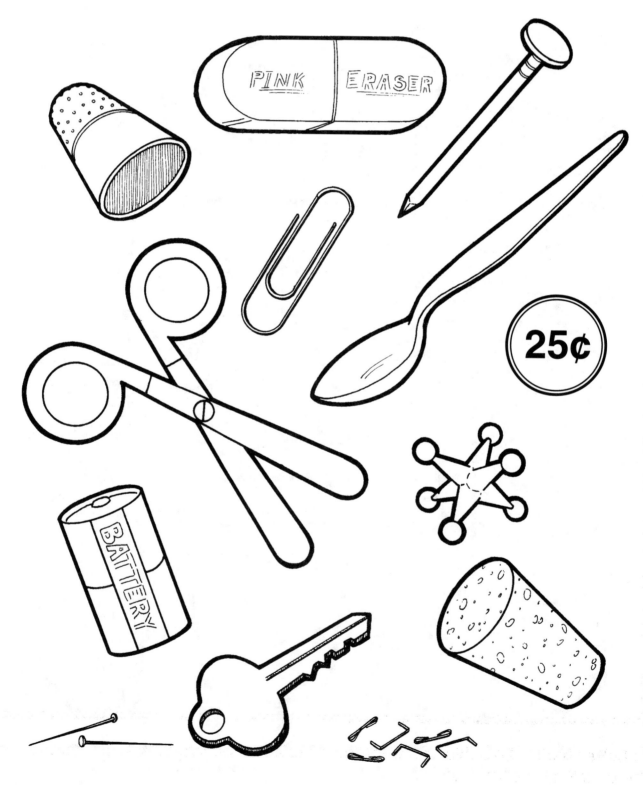

Puzzles

Puzzle Frame

Teacher Note: Use this frame for the puzzles on pages 41–44, or reproduce the puzzles on cardstock.

Puzzles *(cont.)*

Puzzle Pattern

Teacher Note: Have each student draw a picture or write his or her name on the puzzle pattern. Or, program the pattern to use with sight words, number words, color words, or spelling words.

Puzzles *(cont.)*

Three-Piece Puzzle: Spider

Directions: Color and cut out the puzzle pieces. Glue them onto the puzzle frame, making a complete picture.

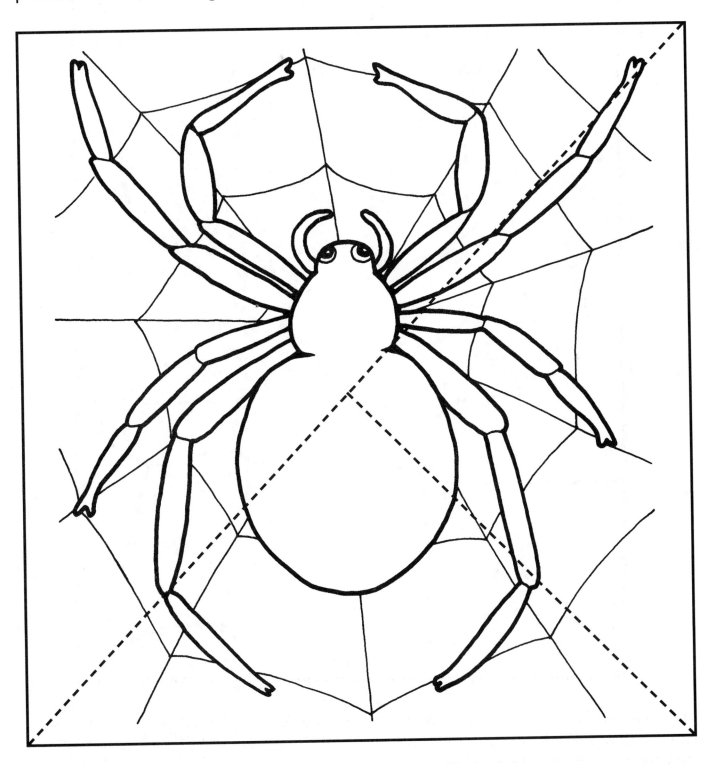

Puzzles *(cont.)*

Six-Piece Puzzle: Monster

Directions: Color and cut out the puzzle pieces. Glue them onto the puzzle frame, making a complete picture.

Puzzles *(cont.)*

Six-Piece Puzzle: Lion

Directions: Color and cut out the puzzle pieces. Glue them onto the puzzle frame, making a complete picture.

Puzzles (cont.)

Six-Piece Puzzle: Mermaid

Directions: Color and cut out the puzzle pieces. Glue them onto the puzzle frame, making a complete picture.

Puzzles (cont.)

Shape Up: Square

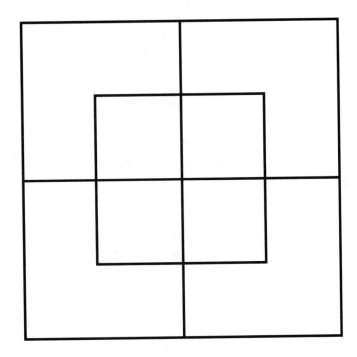

- -

Directions: Cut out the puzzle pieces below on the dashed lines.
Glue them together to make the square above.

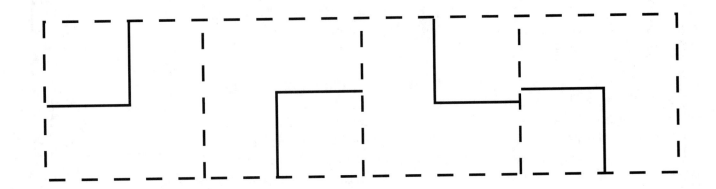

Skills Practice

Paper Cup Stack-Up

Label Styrofoam® cups with the letters of the alphabet, ordinal words, or numbers (to count by twos), etc. Write each label on the outside rim of the cup, close to the bottom. Store each stack-up activity separately in a resealable, plastic bag.

A student selects a bag containing a stack-up activity. He or she lays out all of the Styrofoam cups, then stacks the cups by placing one on top of another to progress through the alphabet, ordinal words, or counting by twos. Direct him or her to complete one set of Styrofoam stacks and put it away before getting out another set.

In addition, paper cup stack-up activities can be developed for rhyming words, counting by fives and tens, etc. Two or more sets of cups containing rhyming words may be mixed together. (For example, one set of cups can be labeled *cat*, *rat*, *sat*, and *bat*, and another set can be labeled *hit*, *pit*, *sit*, and *bit*.) All cups are placed in a bag; the child sets them on the table, then stacks each cup in the appropriate tower of rhyming words. This activity can be made self-checking by numbering the cups on the inside. Children can check to see if the numbers are in the correct order.

Rubber Band Cards

Make rubber band cards by cutting heavy white cardboard into 5" x 7" (13 cm x 18 cm) pieces. Photocopy the card patterns on pages 47–49 and glue each one on a piece of cardboard or create your own to correspond with current classroom skills. On the front, draw five pictures down the right side or use the art on page 50–51 to create your own cards. On the left, write a corresponding skill. Cut out five notches on both the left and right sides of the card. On the back, draw dotted lines for self-checking, connecting the correct items. (These dotted lines will be covered when the rubber bands correctly connect each picture with the appropriate match.) Store each rubber band card and five rubber bands in a resealable, plastic bag. Rubber band cards can be created for a variety of skills including beginning and ending sounds, blends, and math facts.

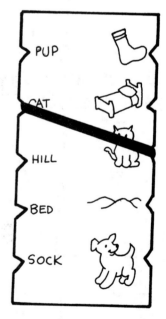

A student looks at the words on the left and the pictures on the right side of the card. Then he or she takes one rubber band, slips it around the card, and puts it in the notch by the word on the left. Finally the student places the other end of the rubber band in the notch on the right by the matching picture. Children use each of the five rubber bands to match the word on the left side to the picture on the right side.

Skills Practice *(cont.)*

Short Vowel Rubber Band Card

pup

cat

hill

bed

sock

Skills Practice *(cont.)*

Long Vowel Rubber Band Card

bee

mice

mule

baby

boat

Skills Practice *(cont.)*

Rubber Band Card Pattern

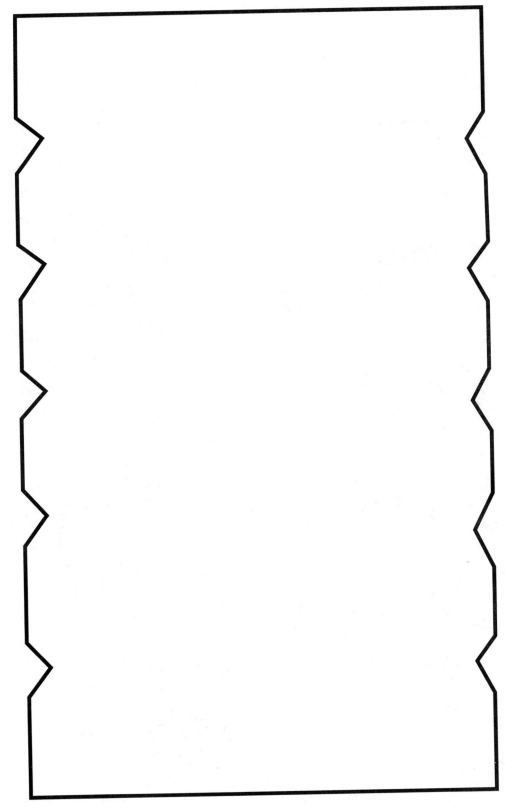

Skills Practice (cont.)

Rubber Band Card Art

Skills Practice *(cont.)*

Rubber Band Card Art *(cont.)*

Play Dough

Playing with dough is an enjoyable way to build motor skills by strengthening children's hands and finger dexterity. There are many things they can do using play dough. You may use store-bought play dough, or you may make your own. (See pages 233–237 for a variety of recipes.) Different play dough recipes offer variations of texture and stiffness.

Use the following activities with students as they play with dough:

- Cut the play dough with scissors.

- Demonstrate how to flatten a piece of play dough. Begin with your hands. If you have a rolling pin available, demonstrate how to use it to flatten a piece of play dough. If you do not have a rolling pin available, a full soup can works well.

- Experiment squeezing the play dough.

- Provide cookie cutters for children to cut shapes in the play dough. Alternatives to cookie cutters include: plastic cups, plastic container lids, plastic knives, and spoons.

- Roll small pieces into "snakes" using the palm of one hand and a flat surface. Provide plastic knives or plastic spoons and allow the children to experiment cutting the rolled play dough.

- Sqeeze play dough through a garlic press.

- Use play dough "snakes" to form letters, numbers, or shapes.

Play Dough *(cont.)*

Play Dough Balls

Have each student make a ball by rolling a little play dough between both palms. As a student becomes skilled at using both hands to make a ball, have him or her roll the play dough into a ball using only the thumb, index finger, and middle finger (the ring finger and little finger are held into the palm). **Hint:** Have students try this on a table surface first. As they become more skilled at making balls, have them hold their hands in the air (not on the table surface) while making the balls. In addition, students can pick up play dough balls using toothpicks.

Play Dough Letters

Make 10–15 play dough balls. Use the balls to form letters, numbers, or shapes. If young students cannot visualize a letter, number, or shape, you may wish to write it on a sheet of paper. Students can use the pencil marks as guides for where to place the balls. Have each student use his or her thumb, index finger, and middle finger to press each ball into a mat. Once the shape has been formed, have each student use the index finger and middle finger to "walk" along the play dough ball. Each student should hold his or her ring finger and little finger with the thumb. The student can flatten the ball with the palm of his or her hand when finished.

Planting Seeds

Provide a small ball of play dough and five beans for each student. Have the student pretend to plant seeds in the play dough. Then, using the pointer finger, he or she pushes beans in one at a time and covers them up with the play dough. After the seeds have been planted, the student squeezes the play dough and finds the five seeds, then takes them out. He or she rolls the play dough back into a ball and lines up the five seeds.

Play Dough *(cont.)*

Play Dough Pictures

Laminate the background patterns on pages 90–93 and allow the children to create animals, people, and objects out of play dough to use in decorating the pages. Encourage the children to make up a story to go along with their picture.

Hide and Seek

Hide objects in the play dough and have the children find them. Pennies, small toys, and beans are small enough to be hidden in the play dough, yet readily discovered by children.

Colorful Play Dough

Drop some food coloring in each student's play dough. A student kneads the play dough using his or her hands until all the color is mixed in the dough. Try adding sprinkles or glitter; then have the student knead the items into the play dough. Or, give each student two balls of different-colored play dough (red, yellow, or blue). Have him or her knead the play dough together to create a secondary color.

Button Stack

Place a toothpick, or piece of uncooked spaghetti, into a ball or lump of play dough. Then have each student stack buttons (with large holes) onto it. This requires hand/eye coordination as well as patience.

Finger Play

Teaching students finger plays is a wonderful way to practice finger dexterity. Usually the students' fingers and/or hands are the characters in the finger play. Students have to manipulate their fingers in order to tell the story in the song or poem. While students may be slow at first, with a little practice, they can recite the song or poem with increasing speed, using their fingers to tell the story. The easiest way to perform finger plays is with the fingers; however, you may want to try some of the following creative ways to spice up the stories.

Note: *The traditional finger plays included in this book are from the oral tradition and cannot be attributed to specific authors.*

Sticker Characters

Purchase mini-dot stickers to use as the characters for the finger plays. Mini-dot stickers feature almost any animal and even some people (especially community helpers). Place the mini-dot stickers on the pads of children's fingers and allow them to do the finger play with the mini-dot "puppets." Consider using colored dot labels with a face drawn on them. For example, green dots with a face can be frogs.

Paper Finger Puppets

Many of the finger plays in this book have patterns next to them which can be reproduced to make puppets. Using cardstock will provide more durability for each puppet. Cut out the finger puppet and have students add details with crayons, colored pencils, paint, or markers. Tape the finger puppets around the children's fingers. Attach larger puppets to 35 mm film canisters using double-stick tape.

Finger Puppet Gloves

Create an easy finger puppet glove by attaching Velcro® to the underside of each fingertip of a gardening glove. Cut out felt figures (the felt will stick to the Velcro). Wear the glove as you perform the finger play that corresponds to the puppet. A more elaborate finger puppet glove can be made by purchasing various colored pompoms to use as the head of each character. Glue googlie eyes to pompoms and draw a mouth with a permanent marker. Cut clothing or body coverings out of felt or fabric. Glue the felt and the pompoms to a gardening glove.

Traditional Finger Plays

Pat-A-Cake

Pat-a-cake, pat-a-cake, baker's man,
(Slap hands on your knees, then clap together three times.)
Bake me a cake just as fast as you can.
(Pretend to be stirring.)
Pat it,
(Clap your hands together.)
Shape it,
(Form hands into a circle.)
And mark it with a B,
(Pretend to write the letter B.)
And put it in the oven for baby and me.
(Pretend to put a cake in an oven.)

Where Is Thumbkin?

Where is thumbkin?
(Hide both hands behind your back.)
Where is thumbkin?
Here I am,
(Bring right hand from behind your back and wiggle thumb.)
Here I am.
(Bring left hand from behind your back and wiggle thumb as if "talking" to the right thumb.)
Very nice to see you,
(Wiggle right thumb.)
Very nice indeed sir.
(Wiggle left thumb.)
Run away,
(Hide right hand behind your back again.)
Run away.
(Hide left hand behind your back again.)
(Repeat using pointer finger, middle finger, ring finger, and pinkie in place of thumbkin.)

Five Little Speckled Frogs

Five little speckled frogs sitting on a speckled log.
(Hold up five fingers.)
Eating some most delicious bugs, yum, yum.
(Rub your belly.)
One jumped into the pool, where it was nice and cool,
(One finger, jumping in pool—other arm rounded.)
Then there were four speckled frogs, glump, glump.
(All say, "Glump, glump.")
(Continue with four, three . . . etc., until there are no frogs left.)

Traditional Finger Plays *(cont.)*

Itsy, Bitsy Spider

The itsy, bitsy spider went up the water spout,

(Use first two fingers to walk up the other arm.)

Down came the rain and washed the spider out.

(Flutter fingers down.)

Out came the sun and dried up all the rain.

(Make circle over head with your arms.)

And the itsy, bitsy spider went up the spout again.

(Use first two fingers to walk up the other arm.)

Baby Bumblebee

I'm bringing home a baby bumblebee.

(Cup one hand over the palm of other hand.)

Won't my mommy be so proud of me?

(Move hands up and down, holding hands as above.)

I'm bringing home a baby bumble bee.

(Continue the action above.)

Ouch! He stung me!

(Open up hands.)

The Apple Tree

Away up high in an apple tree,

(Raise your arms high.)

Two red apples smiled at me.

(Smile and hold up two fingers.)

I shook that tree as hard as I could;

(Shake your hands.)

Down came those apples,

(Bring your hands down.)

And mmmmm, were they good.

(Rub your tummy.)

Three Cornered Hat

My hat, it has three corners,

(Use your thumbs and pointer fingers to form a triangle.)

Three corners has my hat.

(Hold up three fingers.)

A hat without three corners,

(Use your thumbs and pointer fingers to form a triangle.)

Could never be my hat.

(Shake pointer finger to indicate "no.")

Traditional Finger Plays *(cont.)*

Two Little Hands So Clean and Bright

Two little hands so clean and bright.

(Hold up your hands.)

This is my left and this is my right.

(Point to each hand.)

This Old Man

This old man, he played one,

(Hold up appropriate number of fingers.)

He played knick-knack on his thumb.

(Tap your thumbs together.)

Chorus: With a knick-knack, paddy-whack, give a dog a bone,

(Make right hand into fist, point thumb over shoulder.)

This old man came rolling home.

(Roll your hands, one over the other.)

(Repeat actions after each line; repeat chorus after each verse.)

This old man, he played two,
He played knick-knack on his shoe.
This old man, he played three,
He played knick-knack on his knee.
This old man, he played four,
He played knick-knack on the door.
This old man, he played five,
He played knick-knack on his hive.
This old man, he played six,
He played knick-knack on his sticks.
This old man, he played seven,
He played knick-knack up to heaven.
This old man, he played eight,
He played knick-knack on his plate.
This old man, he played nine,
He played knick-knack on his spine.
This old man, he played ten,
He played knick-knack now and then.

Thematic Finger Plays

Cats

This Kitty

(Start by holding up all five fingers on your right hand.)

This kitty said, "I smell a mouse."

(Take one finger away.)

This kitty said, "Let's hunt through the house."

(Take the next finger away.)

This kitty said, "Lets go creepy creep."

(Take the next finger away.)

This kitty said, "Is the mouse asleep?"

(Take the next finger away.)

This kitty said, "Meow, meow,
I saw him go through this hole just now."

(On the last line, run the final finger through a hole made by the left hand.)

Five Little Kittens

Five little kittens standing in a row,

(Hold up five fingers.)

They nod their heads to the children so.

(Bend your fingers.)

They run to the left; they run to the right.

(Run your fingers to the left and then to the right.)

They stand up and stretch in the bright sunlight.

(Stretch your fingers out tall.)

Along comes a dog that's in for some fun.

(Hold up one finger from opposite hand.)

ME-OW! See those little kittens run!

(Make your fingers run.)

Extension: Kitty Ear Headband
Help each child cut out two cat ears from construction paper. Glue the ears onto a 2" (5 cm) wide band that fits the child's head. Let the students wear their headbands as they sing, "This Kitty" and "Five Little Kittens."

Thematic Finger Plays (cont.)

Dogs

Two Little Puppy Dogs

Two little puppy dogs

(Hold up two fingers.)

Lying in a heap,

(Let two fingers fall down.)

Soft and woolly

(Pet two fingers with opposite hand.)

And fast asleep.

(Lay hands against the side of your face and close eyes.)

Along came a pussycat creeping near,

(Hold up one finger from opposite hand and move toward the two fingers.)

"Meow," she cried right into their ears.

Two little puppy dogs

(Hold up two fingers.)

After one cat,

(Two fingers chase the one finger.)

Did you ever play tag like that?

(Point to the children.)

This Little Doggie

(Start by holding up five fingers.)

This little doggie ran away to play.

(Take one finger away.)

This little doggie said, "I'll go too some day."

(Take next finger away.)

This little doggie began to dig and dig.

(Pretend to dig with next finger, then take it away.)

This little doggie danced a funny jig.

(Pretend to dance with next finger, then take it away.)

This little doggie cried, "Ki! Yi! Ki! Yi!
I wish I were big."

(Take the last finger away.)

Extension: Paper-Plate Dog

Have each child make a paper-plate dog. Have him or her cut two dog ears from construction paper. The child draws a dog's face on the paper plate, then glues one ear on each side of the plate.

Thematic Finger Plays *(cont.)*

Fish

Goldfish

My darling little goldfish

(Wiggle one finger.)

Hasn't any toes.

(Point to your toes.)

He swims around without a sound,

(Move fingers in a swimming motion.)

And bumps his hungry nose.

(Point to your nose.)

He can't get out to play with me

(Point to yourself.)

Nor I get in to him.

(Point to children.)

And when I say, "Come out and play,"

(Move fingers to signal, "Come out.")

He says, "Come in and swim."

(Pretend you are swimming.)

I Caught a Fish Alive

One, two, three, four, five,

(Hold up each of five fingers, one at a time.)

I caught a fish alive.

(Imitate holding up the fish.)

Six, seven, eight, nine, ten,

(Lift up each of the fingers of your other hand.)

I let it go again.

(Imitate throwing the fish back.)

Why did I let it go?

(Hold up hands, looking puzzled.)

Because it bit my finger so!

(Shake right hand.)

Which finger did it bite?

(Hold up right hand.)

The little finger on the right.

(Hold up little finger.)

Extension: Fish and Fish Bowl

Cut off about 2" (5 cm) around a paper plate to form a fish bowl. Each child draws colored fish or cuts them from construction paper. He or she glues the fish to the paper plate. For a variation on this activity, have each student glue fish-shaped crackers to the plate.

Thematic Finger Plays *(cont.)*

Birds

I Saw a Little Bird

Once I saw a little bird,
Come hop, hop, hop.

(Make one finger go up and down.)

So I cried,
"Little bird, will you stop, stop, stop?"

(Hold up your hand to signal, "Stop.")

I was going to the window to say
"Howdy-do, Howdy-do."

(Wave hello.)

But he shook his little tail,
and away he flew, flew, flew.

(Move your hands up and down as if flying.)

Five Little Robins

Five little robins in a sycamore tree,

(Hold up five fingers.)

A father,

(Hold up your thumb.)

A mother,

(Hold up pointer finger.)

And babies three.

(Hold up remaining fingers.)

Father brought a worm,

(Point to your thumb.)

Mother brought a bug,

(Point to pointer finger.)

The three baby robins started to tug.

(Make tugging motion with hand.)

This one ate the bug,

(Point to middle finger.)

This one ate the worm,

(Point to ring finger.)

This one sat and waited for his turn.

(Point to little finger.)

Blackbirds

Two little blackbirds sitting on a hill,

(Hold up index fingers.)

One named Jack and one named Jill.

(Bend one finger at a time.)

Fly away Jack.

(Move right hand behind your back.)

Fly away Jill.

(Move left hand behind your back.)

Come back Jack.

(Bring right hand back to front.)

Come back Jill.

(Bring left hand back to front.)

Extension: Seed Collage
Explain to students that birds like to eat seeds. Then provide different types of seeds for each child to glue onto construction paper to create a collage.

Thematic Finger Plays *(cont.)*

Apples

Five Red Apples

Five red apples hanging in a tree,

(Hold up appropriate number of fingers.)

The juiciest apples you ever did see.

The wind came by and gave an angry frown,

(Flutter your fingers downward.)

And one little apple came tumbling down.

(One finger falls.)

Four red apples, hanging in a tree.

(Repeat the poem, using the same actions until no apples are left.)

Teacher Note: This poem can be adapted for children to count down from ten apples.

Dancing Apples

Four little apples dancing in a tree,

(Let four fingers dance.)

They danced so long that they set themselves free.

(Fingers fall.)

They continued to dance as they fell to the ground.

And there by some children these apples were found.

"Oh! Look at the rosy one!

(Hold up first finger.)

It almost bounced!"

"I'll take the red one!"

(Hold up second finger.)

Another announced.

The third child laughed as he chose the yellow one.

(Hold up third finger.)

"I'll take it to Mother, 'cause she lets me have fun."

The fourth child put the last one on a tray,

(Put fourth finger in the palm of your left hand.)

And carefully carried the green apple away.

Extension: Pretend To Be Worms
Children can wiggle on the floor like worms. Make a large apple cutout from poster board or cardboard. Cut the hole large enough for each child to take a turn crawling through it.

Thematic Finger Plays (cont.)

Squirrels

Squirrels in a Tree

Five little squirrels sitting in a tree.
(Hold up five fingers.)
This little squirrel said,
(Hold up one finger.)
"These nuts are for me."
(Point to yourself.)
This little squirrel said,
(Hold up another finger.)
"I like to eat."
(Pretend to eat.)
This little squirrel said,
(Hold up another finger.)
"Nuts are a treat."
(Rub your tummy.)
This little squirrel said,
(Hold up another finger.)
"Do you want some?"
(Point to the children.)
This little squirrel said,
(Hold up your thumb.)
"You may have one."
(Point to a child.)
Five little squirrels went bob, bob, bob.
(Bend your fingers.)
Five little squirrels went nod, nod, nod.
(Bend your wrist.)
Five little squirrels went patter, patter, patter.
(Wiggle your fingers.)
Five little squirrels went chatter, chatter, chatter.
(Move your fingers in a talking motion.)
Five little squirrels scolded you and me
(Shake your finger back and forth.)
As they sat and ate nuts in the big, tall tree.
(Pretend to eat nuts.)

Extension: Forest Animals
Children can pretend to be different forest animals. Have children make the sounds and motions of forest animals.

Thematic Finger Plays *(cont.)*

Halloween

One, Two, Three Little Witches

One little, two little, three little witches

(Hold up one, two, then three fingers.)

Fly over haystacks, fly over ditches,

(Make three fingers fly.)

Slide down moonbeams without any hitches,

(Slide fingers down.)

Heigh-ho! Halloween's here!

A Little Witch

A little witch in a pointed cap,

(Make hands into a point over your head.)

On my door went rap, rap, rap.

(Pretend to knock on a door.)

When I went to open it,

(Pretend to open the door.)

She was not there;

(Hold your hands outward.)

She was riding a broomstick,

(Fork two fingers over the pointer finger of left hand.)

High up in the air.

(Hold your fingers high in the air.)

The Ghost

See my great big scary eyes.

(Circle fingers around your eyes.)

Look out now for a big surprise.

(Raise your hands in surprise.)

Oo-oo-oo

I'm looking right at you.

(Point to the children.)

Boo!

Thematic Finger Plays *(cont.)*

Halloween *(cont.)*

Five Little Pumpkins

Five little pumpkins sitting on a gate,

(Hold up five fingers.)

The first one said, "Oh my, it's getting late."

(Hold up first finger.)

The second one said,

"There are witches in the air."

(Hold up second finger.)

The third one said, "I don't care."

(Hold up third finger.)

The fourth one said, ""Let's run, run, run."

(Hold up fourth finger.)

The fifth one said, "It's Halloween fun."

(Hold up fifth finger.)

Then woooooooo went the wind,

(Let five fingers swoosh through the air.)

And out went the light!

(Fold five fingers under.)

Five little pumpkins rolled out of sight.

(Roll one hand over the other.)

Very Nice Jack-O'-Lantern

This is the very nice jack-o'-lantern,

(Hold your hands to form a circle.)

These are the eyes of the jack-o'-lantern.

(Use your thumbs and pointer fingers to form a triangle.)

This is the nose of the jack-o'-lantern.

(Use your thumbs and pointer fingers to form a triangle.)

This is the mouth of the jack-o'-lantern.

(Use pointer finger to draw a smile.)

And this is where the candle goes.

(Use one hand to form a circle. Use pointer finger of the other hand to point to the middle of the circle.)

Thematic Finger Plays *(cont.)*

Thanksgiving

Five Little Pilgrims

Five little Pilgrims on Thanksgiving Day,

(Hold up five fingers.)

The first one said, "I'll have cake if I may."

(Wiggle your thumb.)

The second one said, "I'll have turkey roasted."

(Wiggle next finger.)

The third one said, "I'll have chestnuts toasted."

(Wiggle next finger.)

The fourth one said, "I'll have pumpkin pie."

(Wiggle next finger.)

The fifth one said, "Oh, cranberries I spy."

(Wiggle your pinkie.)

But before the Pilgrims ate their turkey dressing,

They bowed their heads and said a Thanksgiving blessing.

(Bow your head.)

Five Little Turkeys

Five little turkeys standing in a row,

(Hold up five fingers.)

First little turkey said, "I don't want to grow."

(Wiggle your thumb.)

Second little turkey said, "Why do you say that?

(Wiggle next finger.)

Third little turkey said, "I want to get fat."

(Wiggle next finger.)

Fourth little turkey said, "Thanksgiving is near."

(Wiggle next finger.)

Fifth little turkey said, "Yes, that's what I hear."

(Wiggle your pinkie.)

Then the five little turkeys that were standing in a row,

All said together, "Come on, let's GO!"

(Run fingers away.)

Thematic Finger Plays (cont.)

Snow

Ten Little Snowmen

Ten little snowmen dressed up fine;
(Hold up ten fingers.)
This one melted, and then there were nine.
(Bend down one finger.)
Nine little snowmen standing tall and straight;
(Show nine fingers.)
This one melted, and then there were eight.
(Bend down one finger.)
Eight little snowmen white as clouds in heaven;
(Show eight fingers.)
This one melted, and then there were seven.
(Bend down one finger.)
Seven little snowmen with arms made of sticks;
(Show seven fingers.)
This one melted, and then there were six.
(Bend down one finger.)
Six little snowmen looking so alive;
(Show six fingers.)
This one melted, and then there were five.
(Bend down one finger.)
Five little snowmen with mittens from the store;
(Show five fingers.)
This one melted, and then there were four.
(Bend down one finger.)
Four little snowmen beneath a green pine tree;
(Show four fingers.)
This one melted, and then there were three.
(Bend down one finger.)
Three little snowmen with pipes and mufflers, too;
(Show three fingers.)
This one melted, and then there were two.
(Bend down one finger.)
Two little snowmen standing in the sun;
(Show two fingers.)
This one melted, and then there was one.
(Bend down one finger.)
One little snowman started to run,
(Show one finger.)
But he melted away, and then there were none.
(Bend down last finger.)

The Snow

This is the way the snow comes down,
(Flutter your fingers downward.)
Upon a winter day,
(Wrap arms around your body as if it were cold.)
But soon the golden sun comes out,
(Hold arms in a circle above your head.)
And melts it all away.
(Pretend to melt away.)

Thematic Finger Plays *(cont.)*

Snow *(cont.)*

I Built a Little Snowman

I built a little snowman.

(Make a circle with your hands.)

He had a carrot nose.

(Point to your nose.)

Along came a bunny.

(Hold up first two fingers on one hand, slightly bent.)

And what do you suppose?

That hungry little bunny,

(Make a bunny again.)

Looking for his lunch,

(Hop the bunny around.)

Ate the snowman's nose.

(Pretend the bunny is eating your nose.)

Nibble! Nibble! Crunch!

(Pretend to eat a carrot.)

I Am a Snowman

I am a snowman, cold and white.

(Make a circle with each hand, and put one hand on top of the other.)

I stand so still all through the night.

(Hold your hands still, on top of each other.)

I have a carrot nose way up high,

(Point to your nose.)

And a lump of coal to make each eye.

(Point to your eyes.)

I have a muffler made of red,

(Point to your neck.)

And a stovepipe hat upon my head.

(Point to the top of your head.)

Extension: Pretend To Be Snowflakes

Have children move around the room pretending to be snowflakes. Let them lazily drift down to the ground. For an alternative activity, have students practice folding and cutting paper to make snowflakes.

Thematic Finger Plays (cont.)

Valentines

Five Little Valentines

One little valentine said, "I love you."

(Hold up one finger.)

Tommy✶ made another; then there were two.

(Hold up two fingers.)

Two little valentines, one for me.

Mary✶ made another; then there were three.

(Hold up three fingers.)

Three little valentines said,
"We need one more."

Johnny✶ made another; then there were four.

(Hold up four fingers.)

Four little valentines, one more to arrive.

Susan made another; then there were five.

(Hold up five fingers.)

Five little valentines, all ready to say,

(Move five fingers in a talking motion.)

"Be my valentine on this happy day."

✶ *Insert different children's names.*

Valentine's Good Morning

Good morning to you, Valentine,

(Point to a child.)

Curl your locks as I do mine.

(Point to your hair.)

Two before, and three behind.

(Hold up two fingers in front of your shoulders; then hold three fingers behind shoulders.)

Good morning to you, Valentine.

(Point to a child.)

Extension: Lace Valentines

Have each child sew two paper lace hearts together with yarn and plastic yarn needles. Direct him or her to leave a small opening to stuff it with cotton balls that have been sprayed with perfume. Then the child finishes sewing and ties the ends together into a bow. Punch a hole at the top and attach yarn so it can be displayed. Write, "Happy Valentine's Day," on the valentine using a fine tip permanent marker.

Thematic Finger Plays *(cont.)*

Pigs

Five Little Pigs

"Let us go to the woods," said this little pig.

(Hold up your thumb.)

"What to do there?" says that little pig.

(Hold up first finger.)

"To look for my mother," says this little pig.

(Hold up middle finger.)

"What to do with her?" says that little pig.

(Hold up ring finger.)

"Give her a kiss," says this little pig.

(Hold up little finger.)

Two Mother Pigs

Two mother pigs lived in a pen,

(Hold up both thumbs.)

Each had four babies, and that made ten.

(Hold up ten fingers.)

These four babies were as black as night,

(Hold up four fingers on one hand.)

These four babies were black and white.

(Hold up four fingers on other hand.)

But all eight babies loved to play,

(Hold up eight fingers.)

And they rolled and rolled in the mud all day.

(Roll one hand over the other.)

At night, with their mothers, they curled up in a heap,

(Make a fist with each hand.)

And squealed and squealed till they went to sleep.

(Put your cheek on your hand.)

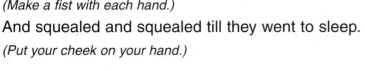

Extension: Plate Pig

Have each child cut out two ears and glue them onto the top of a paper plate. If desired, the child can add facial features using crayons or markers.

Thematic Finger Plays *(cont.)*

Rabbits

Little Bunny Foo Foo

Little Bunny Foo Foo,

(Hold up first two fingers, slightly bent.)

Hopping through the forest,

(Make the bunny hop.)

Scooping up the field mice

(Scoop up mice.)

And bopping them on the head!

(Hit one hand against the other fist.)

Down came the good fairy and said,

(Hold fingers up in the air and move them downward.)

"Little Bunny Foo Foo,

(Hold up first two fingers, slightly bent.)

I don't like your attitude—

(Point finger from other hand at the bunny.)

Scooping up the field mice

(Scoop up mice.)

And bopping them on the head.

(Hit one hand against the other fist.)

I'll give you three chances

(Hold up three fingers.)

And if you don't behave,

(Point finger from other hand at the bunny.)

I'll turn you into a GOON!"

(Put a thumb in each ear and flutter your fingers.)

(Repeat the poem three times until three chances are gone. Continue with the same movements. Then add the last stanza.)

And on the fourth day the fairy came and said,

"Little Bunny Foo Foo,

I gave you three chances.

And you still didn't behave.

Now I'll turn you into a GOON!"

Thematic Finger Plays *(cont.)*

Rabbits *(cont.)*

Five Little Rabbits

Five little rabbits sitting by the door,
(Hold up five fingers.)
One hopped away, and then there were four.
(Move one finger, hopping away.)
Hop, hop, hop, hop, see how they run!
(Continue hopping.)
Hop, hop, hop, hop, they think it's great fun!
(Continue hopping.)
Four little rabbits under a tree,
(Hold up four fingers.)
One hopped away, and then there were three.
(Move one finger, hopping away.)
Hop, hop, hop, hop, see how they run!
(Continue hopping.)
Hop, hop, hop, hop, they think it's great fun!
(Continue hopping.)
Three little rabbits looking at you,
(Hold up three fingers.)
One hopped away, and then there were two.
(Move one finger, hopping away.)
Hop, hop, hop, hop, see how they run!
(Continue hopping.)
Hop, hop, hop, hop, they think it's great fun!
(Continue hopping.)
Two little rabbits resting in the sun,
(Hold up two fingers.)
Hop, hop, hop, hop, see how they run!
(Continue hopping.)
Hop, hop, hop, hop, they think it's great fun!
(Continue hopping.)
One little rabbit left all alone,
(Hold up one finger.)
He hopped away, and then there were none.
(Move one finger, hopping away.)
Hop, hop, hop, hop, see how they run!
(Continue hopping.)
Hop, hop, hop, hop, they think it's great fun!
(Continue hopping.)

Extension: Hop like a Bunny
Let each child pretend to hop like a bunny. Have him or her hop on two feet, then hop on one.

Thematic Finger Plays *(cont.)*

The Garden

My Garden

This is my garden. I'll rake it with care.

(Pretend to rake.)

And then some flower seeds I'll plant there.

(Pretend to plant seeds.)

The sun will shine,

(Put arms over your head in a circle.)

And the rain will fall,

(Put your hands in the air and bring them down as rain.)

Any my garden will blossom and grow straight and tall.

(Make a fist, then open it up slowly like a blooming flower.)

Dig a Little Hole

Dig a little hole.

(Pretend to dig a hole.)

Plant a little seed.

(Use your thumb and pointer finger to pretend to plant a seed.)

Pour a little water.

(Pretend to use a watering can to water the seed.)

And pull a little weed.

(Pretend to pull the weed.)

Extension: Feeling Fruits and Vegetables
Place a variety of fruits and vegetables on a table or in a basket. Encourage the children to "touch and feel" the textures on the various fruits and vegetables.

Thematic Finger Plays (cont.)

Farms

The Farmer
First the farmer sows his seeds,

(Pretend to sow seeds.)

Then he stands and takes his ease.

He stamps his foot.

(Stamp your foot.)

And claps his hands,

(Clap your hands.)

And turns around to view his lands.

(Put hands over your eyebrows and look to the left and right.)

This Little Cow
This little cow eats grass,

(Hold up your thumb.)

This little cow eats hay,

(Hold up first finger.)

This little cow drinks water,

(Hold up next finger.)

This little cow runs away.

(Hold up next finger.)

This little cow does nothing,

But just lies down all day.

(Hold up your pinkie.)

Five Little Farmers
Five little farmers woke up in the sun,

(Hold up five fingers.)

For it was early in the morning and chores must be done.

The first little farmer went to milk the cow.

(Hold up your thumb.)

The second little farmer thought he'd better plow.

(Hold up first finger.)

The third little farmer fed the hungry hens.

(Hold up next finger.)

The fourth little farmer mended broken pens.

(Hold up next finger.)

The fifth little farmer took his vegetables to town.

(Hold up your pinkie.)

Baskets filled with cabbages, and sweet potatoes brown.

When the work was finished and the western sky was red,

Five little farmers tumbled into bed!

(Hold up five fingers.)

Thematic Finger Plays *(cont.)*

Frogs

Mr. Green Froggie

Mr. Green Froggie was fast asleep,
(Put your cheek on your hand.)
On a lily pad where the pool was deep.
He heard some wings go buzzing by.
(Flap your arms.)
He opened his eyes and there was a fly.
(Open your eyes wide.)
Snap went the froggie!
(Snap your fingers.)
Away the fly flew!
(Flap your arms.)
And Mr. Green Froggie went hopping off, too.
(Hop away.)

Five Little Froggies

Five little froggies sitting on a well,
(Hold up five fingers.)
One peeked in and down he fell.
(Hold up one finger.)
Froggies jumped high.
(With hand, jump high.)
Froggies jumped low.
(With hand, jump low.)
Froggies jumped everywhere, to and fro!
(With both hands, jump forward and sideways.)
(Continue until no frogs are left.)

Mr. Bullfrog

Here's Mr. Bullfrog sitting on a rock.
(Hold up one finger.)
Along comes a little boy;
*(With other hand, use first two fingers to show
a boy walking.)*
Mr. Bullfrog jumps! Kerflop!
(With one finger, jump.)

Extension: Let's Act
Let the children act out the finger play, "Five Little Froggies." The children sit, in groups of
five, on a balance beam or a strip of tape on the floor. As the rest of the class recites the
poem, each group can take a turn acting this out. One "frog" at a time jumps into the pool
until the end of the poem.

Thematic Finger Plays *(cont.)*

Caterpillars

Fuzzy Caterpillar

Fuzzy little caterpillar,

(Hold up your thumb.)

Into a corner will creep.

He'll spin himself a blanket,

(Hide thumb inside your hand.)

And then go fast asleep.

Fuzzy little caterpillar,

Fuzzy little caterpillar,

Wakes up by and by.

To find he has wings,

(Put thumbs beside each other and hold fingers outward.)

And he has turned into a…

Butterfly!

(Hold hands same as above and move fingers.)

Sleepy Caterpillars

"Let's go to sleep," the caterpillars said,

(Hold up your thumbs.)

As they tucked themselves into their beds.

(Hide thumbs inside your hands.)

They will awaken by and by,

(Take thumbs out of your hands.)

And each one will be a beautiful butterfly.

(Put thumbs together and flap hands.)

Extension: Dance like a Butterfly

Using scarves or streamers, encourage children to dance like butterflies. Children can hold streamers in their hands, or you can attach scarves to their shoulders.

Thematic Finger Plays *(cont.)*

Mice

A Mouse Lived in a Hole

A mouse lived in a hole,
(Make a circle with your thumb and index finger.)
Lived softly in a little hole.
(Put index finger of other hand in the hole.)
When all was quiet as can be,
("Sh! Sh!"—put index finger to lips.)
Out popped HE!
(Pop your finger out of the hole.)

This Little Mouse

Five little mice on the pantry floor.
(Hold up five fingers.)
This little mouse peeked behind the door.
(Hold up your thumb.)
This little mouse nibbled at some cake.
(Hold up next finger.)
This little mouse not a sound did make.
(Hold up next finger.)
This little mouse took a bite of cheese.
(Hold up next finger.)
This little mouse heard the kitten sneeze.
(Hold up your pinkie.)
"Ah-choo!" sneezed the kitten.
And "Squeak!" the mice cried, and they found
a hole and ran inside.
(Make a circle with your thumb and index finger; run the fingers of other hand into the hole.)

Hickory Dickory Dock

Hickory dickory dock.
The mouse ran up the clock.
(Use first two fingers, run upward.)
The clock struck one.
(Hold up one finger.)
The mouse ran down.
(Use first two fingers, run back down.)
Hickory dickory dock.

Extension: Heart Mouse

Cut out a large, gray construction-paper heart. (The pointed part of the heart will be the nose of the mouse.) Have each child draw facial features on the mouse, and add a piece of yarn for the tail. Then direct him or her to cut out pink ears and glue them to the side of the mouse's head.

Thematic Finger Plays *(cont.)*

Family

Grandma's Spectacles

These are grandma's spectacles,

(Make circles around your eyes with fingers.)

This is grandma's hat.

(Use both hands and cup them on your head.)

This is the way she folds her hands,

(Fold your hands.)

And puts them in her lap.

(Put hands in your lap.)

Baby Grows

Five little fingers on this hand,

(Hold up five fingers.)

Five little fingers on that.

(Hold up five fingers on the other hand.)

A dear little nose,

(Point to your nose.)

A mouth like a rose.

(Point to your mouth.)

Two little cheeks so tiny and fat.

(Point to your cheeks.)

Two eyes and two ears,

(Point to your eyes, then ears.)

And ten little toes.

(Point to your toes.)

That is the way the baby grows.

Thematic Finger Plays *(cont.)*

Family *(cont.)*

The Family

This is the daddy who bakes the bread,
(Hold up your thumb.)
This is the mother who tucks us into bed.
(Hold up pointer finger.)
This is the brother who cuddles the doll,
(Hold up next finger.)
This is the sister who bounces the ball.
(Hold up next finger.)
This is the baby, the last one of all.
(Hold up your pinkie.)
Oh, how we love them all.
(Wrap your arms around yourself for a hug.)

Good Strong Mother

Good strong mother, how do you do?
(Hold up your thumb.)
Dear strong daddy, glad to see you.
(Hold up next finger.)
Big, tall brother, pleased to see you are here.
(Hold up next finger.)
Kind little sister, you need not fear.
(Hold up next finger.)
Glad welcome we'll give you, and baby dear too,
Yes baby dear, how do you do?
(Hold up your pinkie.)

Extension: A Special Bouquet

Help each child create tissue-paper flowers and attach them to pipe cleaners. He or she can tie a few flowers together in a bouquet with ribbon or yarn. Attach a note for the child's parent or another special person.

Thematic Finger Plays *(cont.)*

Community Helpers

Any Mail for Me?

Five little letters lying on a tray,

(Hold up five fingers.)

Mommy came in and took the first away.

(Take away your pinkie.)

Then Daddy said, "This big one is for me."

(Take away next finger.)

I counted them twice; now there were three.

(Count three fingers.)

Brother Bill asked, "Did I get any mail?"

He found one and cried, "A letter from Gail!"

(Take away next finger.)

My sister Jane took the next to last,

(Take away next finger.)

And ran upstairs to open it fast.

As I can't read, I'm not able to see,

Whom the last one's for, but I hope it's for me! *((Remove your thumb.)*

Extension: Graham Crackers in White Envelopes

Give each child a "special delivery" by placing a graham cracker in a white envelope. Let him or her open the envelope and taste the treat.

Thematic Finger Play *(cont.)*

Community Helpers *(cont.)*

Dentist

If I were a dentist,

(Point to yourself.)

I know what I would do.

I'd tell all the children, "Brush your teeth."

(Imitate brushing your teeth.)

"Keep a smile like new."

(Smile.)

And if a tiny hole should show,

(Make a circle with your fingers.)

I'd say, "Climb into my chair."

I'd make my little drill go buzzz,

(Make a buzzing sound.)

And put a filling there!

(Point to your teeth.)

Miss Polly

Miss Polly had a dolly

Who was sick, sick, sick.

(Pretend to rock a baby.)

She called for the doctor

(Imitate calling on the telephone.)

To come quick, quick, quick.

He came in a hurry

With his bag and his hat.

(Pretend to put on a hat.)

He knocked on the door

(Make a knocking motion.)

With a rat-a-tat-tat.

He looked at the baby

(Cradle your arms.)

And he shook his head.

(Shake your head.)

He said to Miss Polly,

"Put her right to bed."

(Point and shake your finger.)

He wrote on a paper

(Pretend to write.)

For a pill, pill, pill.

"I'll be back in the morning

(Point to yourself.)

With my bill, bill, bill."

(Pretend to wave a piece of paper.)

Thematic Finger Plays *(cont.)*

Around the House

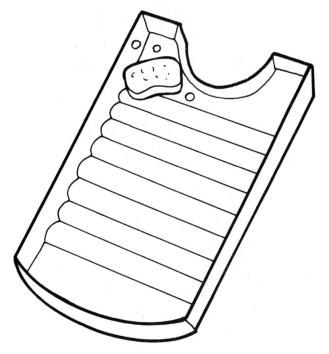

Here's a Little Washboard

Here's a little washboard;
(Hold up palm of your left hand.)
Here's a little tub;
(Make a circle with fingers on your right hand.)
Here's a little cake of soap,
(Make an oval with fingers on the right hand.)
And here's the way we scrub.
(Have fingers go up and down on your left hand.)
Here's a line way up high;
(Draw an imaginary line in the air.)
Now the clothes are drying.
(Wave your fingers back and forth.)
Hear the wind come whistling by;
(Cup hand to your ear.)
See! The clothes are flying.
(Wave your hand harder.)

Shiny Shoes

First I loosen mud and dirt,
(Use one hand to brush the other.)
My shoes I then rub clean,
(Rub one hand.)
For shoes in such a dreadful sight,
(Hide hand behind your back.)
Never should be seen.
And then I spread the polish on,
(Rub one hand.)
And then I let it dry.
I brush and brush, and brush and brush,
(Make fist and brush the hand.)
How those shoes shine! Oh, my!
(Extend your hand and admire.)

Extension: Bars of Soap
Mix soap flakes and water until you have a thick mixture. Then have each child mold his or her own bar of soap. Let him or her try using the soap. Ask the child how it feels.

Sign Language

Teach students hand movements for sign language. You can show them the signs for a simple song or the signs for letters. Students are always excited to learn how to sign their own names. The signs for the letters of the alphabet are shown below.

American Sign Language Alphabet

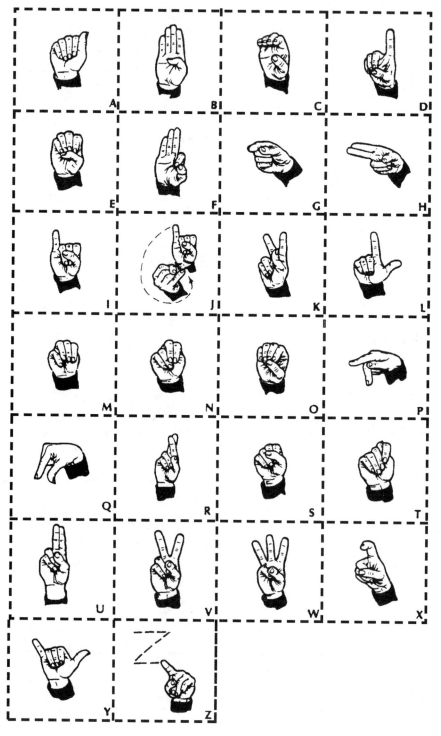

Art Activities

Practice with the interplay of the fingers is important before writing instruments are introduced. Students need strength, dexterity, and coordination in the fingers and thumb before a child will have good coloring, writing, and cutting skills. Activities on this page and pages 86–139 can be used to help students practice bending and extending the fingers and thumb.

Ant Tracks

Provide each child with a white sheet of paper, raisins, and black paint. A child uses the raisins as stamps by dipping the raisins into the paint, and then pressing them on the paper. After the paint dries, he or she uses markers to add legs and antennae to the ants. The child can complete the picture by drawing a habitat for the ants.

Cotton Swab Painting

For an alternative to a paintbrush, allow each child to paint with cotton swabs. Simply provide paint, paper, and cotton swabs. Let him or her create unique paintings. A student can use the cotton swabs to fill in the color on a picture. It is easiest to use a fairly large pattern at first. Reproduce the patterns on pages 86–88, or page 147, or use a coloring book. As he or she becomes skilled at painting with a cotton swab, have him or her try smaller pictures.

Dot Pictures

Use a pencil with an unused eraser at the end of it. A student should hold the pencil so that he or she can dip the eraser into paint or an ink pad. The student uses the end of the eraser as a stamp to create a picture or to decorate with dots. Encourage each student to use his or her thumb and index finger to hold the pencil. A student can fill in the color on a picture using this "dot" technique. Reproduce one of the patterns on pages 86–88, or use a large, basic picture from a coloring book.

Art Activities (cont.)

Balloons

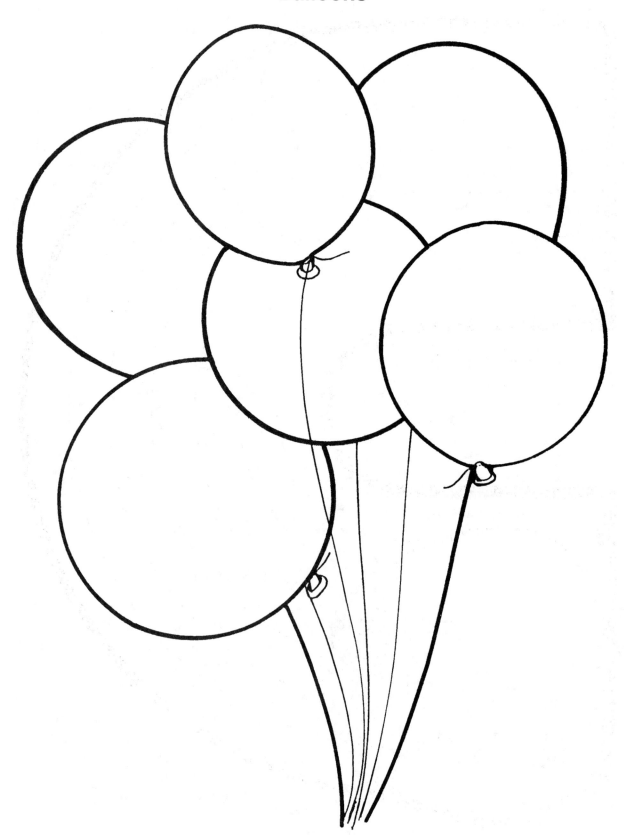

Art Activities *(cont.)*

Rainbow

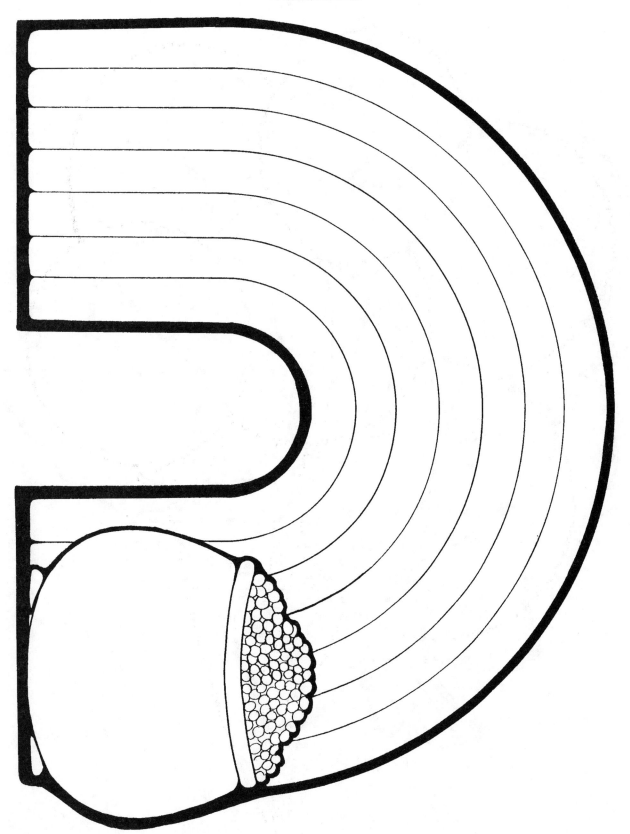

Art Activities *(cont.)*

Flowers

Shape Activities

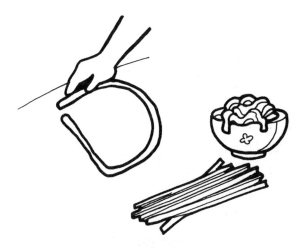

Spaghetti Shapes

Cook spaghetti noodles approximately two minutes less than the recommended package time. Use the spaghetti to form shapes, letters, and numbers. Colored spaghetti adds interest to this activity.

Fingerprint Animals

Provide ink pads for the children. If possible, locate this activity near a sink. A child presses his or her fingers into the ink pad; then presses them onto paper. Have the child use crayons to add legs, eyes, antennae, or other parts to create a fingerprint animal. If they wish each child can cut out his or her animal and then glue it onto a chosen background. See pages 90–91 for habitat patterns.

Additional background patterns can be found on pages 92–93.

Toothpick Shapes

Squeeze some glue onto a piece of wax paper. A child selects a sheet of colored construction paper. He or she dips toothpicks into the glue and makes a geometric design on the paper by gluing down the toothpicks.

To make this activity more complex, specify the number of toothpicks to be used in a design. For example, a child could use exactly 12 toothpicks to make a design with four triangles. Another option is to use one of the sheets provided on pages 94–95 and have the child copy the design on another sheet of paper using toothpicks.

In addition, he or she can use toothpicks to spell out his or her name.

Shape Activities *(cont.)*

Fingerprint Background—Farm

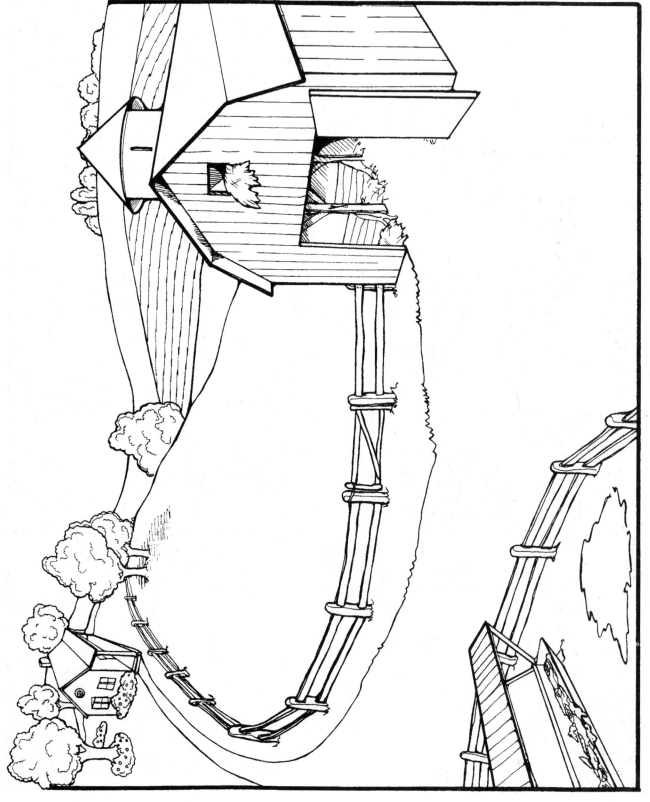

Shape Activities *(cont.)*

Fingerprint Background—Jungle

Shape Activities *(cont.)*

Fingerprint Background—Circus

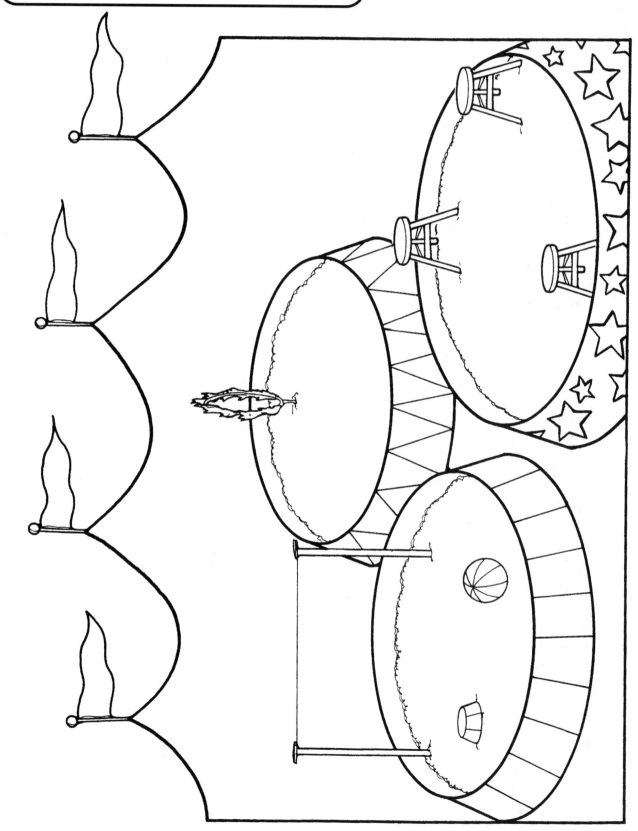

Shape Activities *(cont.)*

Fingerprint Background—Home

Shape Activities *(cont.)*

Toothpick Designs

Shape Activities *(cont.)*

Toothpick Designs *(cont.)*

Pretending Activities

Locks and Keys

Begin with three padlocks (small, medium, and large) on a key ring. Demonstrate how to try a different key in each lock until one works, showing how to open each padlock and take it off the ring. After all the locks have been opened and removed from the key ring, show the children how to lock them back onto the ring. It is not necessary to point out that once a key works for one lock it won't work for the others; let the children discover this for themselves.

Dial It!

Have children practice using their fingers to push the keys on a telephone. Also, students can practice number recognition and counting during this activity. You may call out numbers for students to press or provide index cards with number sequences written on them. If appropriate, create a class book of the children's telephone numbers. Each student practices dialing his or her own phone number or dialing a friend's phone number and pretends to have a conversation. Begin by having the student use his or her index finger. Then, have him or her practice using other fingers as well. If a phone is not available, have the student practice isolating fingers by pretending to press the phone pattern keys on page 97.

Keyboards

Obtain musical keyboards and computer keyboards for students to use. The students will guide themselves through hours of fine motor practice. The keyboards don't have to work, but if they do, it adds to the fun! Or, you can use an old typewriter (explaining what it is can be a lot of fun).

Pretending Activities *(cont.)*

Telephone Pattern

Counting Activities

Bean Count

Open an empty egg carton and label the bottom of each compartment with a number from 1–12. Provide a cup of beans for students to use for counting. A child fills the egg carton compartments by placing the appropriate number of beans in each compartment of the egg carton. For example, if the number in the compartment is 2, the child counts and places 2 beans in that compartment. Encourage the child to use his or her thumb and pointer finger when picking up the beans.

For an extension to this activity, have the child place one bean in the number 1 compartment. Then he or she picks up that bean and moves it to the number 2 compartment. Next, the child picks up the bean and moves it to the number 3 compartment, and continues to move the bean until it reaches the number 12 compartment.

Toothpick Count

Provide a box of toothpicks for students to use for counting. Label 10 index cards, each with a number from 1–10. Place the index cards facedown on a table. A child selects a card; then picks up that many toothpicks. This activity may be turned into a game. Have each child count his or her toothpicks at the end of the activity. The child with the most toothpicks wins the round.

Button Sort

Label each of 7 paper cups with one of the following color words: red, blue, green, pink, yellow, black, and white. The colors should match the colors of the button collection used. Sort the buttons by color. On the bottom of each cup, write the number of buttons that should be placed in it. Put the correct number of each color of buttons in a container. Set the cups on a table. Have each child take out several buttons and sort them, by color, into the cups. Continue to work until all the buttons are sorted.

Encourage the child to use his or her thumb and pointer finger when picking up objects to sort. When all the buttons are in the cups, have the child dump out one cup at a time and count the buttons.

The number on the bottom of the cup should equal the number of buttons in the cup. For example, the cup labeled red may have the number 8 on the bottom. This means there should be 8 red buttons in the cup.

Use the pattern on page 99 as an extension. Label the tree before presenting it to the children. A student sorts the buttons onto the tree branches based on colors, number of holes, or size of the buttons. Use other objects to sort, such as nuts, beans, pasta, and crayons.

Counting Activities (cont.)

Button Tree Pattern

Lacing Activities

Lacing Cards

Trace a pattern onto tagboard. Any simple pattern will work; however, patterns specifically for this activity are provided on pages 101–103. Cut out the shape of the pattern and punch holes around the edges. Give each child a length of yarn that has tape on one end (a shoestring also works). Students use the yarn to "sew" the lacing cards. For ease and durability, it is advisable to laminate the patterns.

Shoelace Sewing Kit

Create your own lacing cards. Gather old magazines and cut out colorful pictures. Then glue the pictures onto poster board. Punch evenly spaced holes, about 1" (2.5 cm) apart, around the entire edge of the poster board. On some of the boards, make the holes farther apart to see what works best for your children.

Find a box large enough to hold the punched picture cards and shoestrings. In place of shoestrings, simply twist the ends of yarn, dip them in white glue, and let them dry. This will form a pointed, strong end and make it easier to push the yarn through the card. Demonstrate how to string the picture cards with the shoestring or yarn. Also try using wrapping paper or leftover greeting cards for sewing practice.

Lollipop Lids

Punch holes in plastic lids from coffee cans or margarine tubs. Create a yarn needle by painting a bit of glue at the end of one end of yarn and allowing it to dry. Secure the other end of the yarn to the lid. A child weaves the yarn in and out of the holes in the lids. To make a lollipop, the teacher uses hot glue to attach a craft stick to the back of the lid.

Lacing Activities *(cont.)*

Lacing Cards

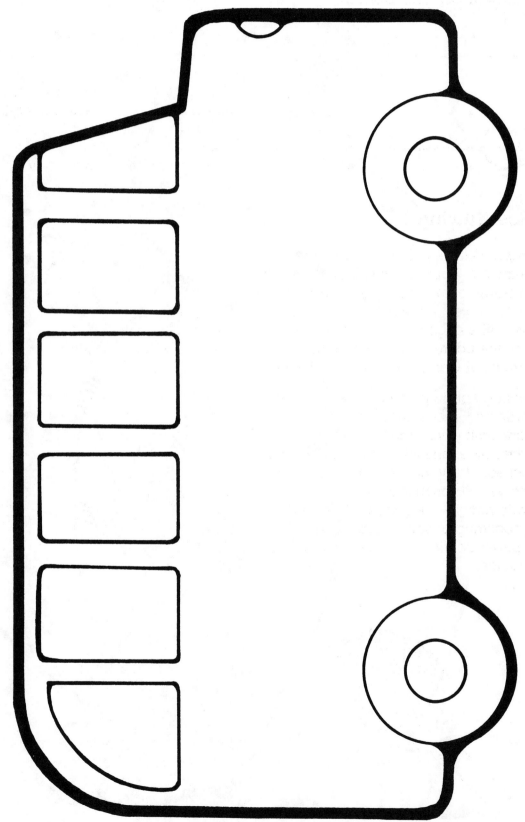

Lacing Activities *(cont.)*

Lacing Cards *(cont.)*

102

Lacing Activities (cont.)

Lacing Cards (cont.)

Stringing Activities

Shoestring Jewelry

Use shoestrings to provide practice stringing objects. If a shoestring is not available, make your own by painting the end of a piece of yarn with glue. When the glue dries it will become a "needle," good for stringing objects. Another option is to tightly wrap tape around one end of a piece of yarn. Buy a variety of "stringable" pasta. Types that will work well for this activity includes salad macaroni (ditalini, elbow, ziti, penne, rigatoni, and wagon wheels). When selecting pasta for this activity, remember that the pasta needs to have a reasonable-sized hole, and should not be too long.

Next, obtain a small plastic container to store each kind of pasta for a shoestring jewelry kit. You can use leftover, clean margarine tubs with lids for this purpose. Using the pasta and a shoestring, demonstrate how to string jewelry. A student ties a large knot in one end of each shoestring. Then he or she uses scissors to cut the other end of the shoestring into different lengths for bracelets, necklaces, etc. (It will help to keep one plastic end on a string to serve as a needle.) Finally, direct the child to thread pasta onto each shoestring. When finished, tie the two ends together.

Other types of objects that can be threaded also work well for this activity. Try beads, cereal, drinking straws cut into pieces, and packing peanuts. If the objects you are using come in different colors or shapes, or if you are using a variety of materials, encourage the students to create patterns while making the necklaces.

For a challenge, have each student string objects on an uncooked piece of spaghetti. (Handle the spaghetti gently; it is delicate before it is cooked.)

Squeezing Activities

Dropping Water

Fill a small cup with colored water. Using thumb, index, and middle finger tips, a student squeezes an eyedropper to fill it with colored water. Then he or she releases one drop of water at a time into small circles drawn on paper. (The student needs to hold his or her arm up so the eyedropper is not touching the paper, but is about 1", or 2.5 cm, above it.) Try using an eyedropper to drop water onto a penny. Challenge each student to see how many drops of water will fit on the penny (without falling off). In addition, each student can see how many drops will fit on a nickel or quarter.

Turkey Baster Races

Place a Ping-Pong ball or cotton ball on the floor. Move the ball along the ground by squeezing the bulb end of a turkey baster. Air will be forced out, moving the ball. Create a game by having two teams compete against each other to race from one point to another point.

Eraser Grips

Any type of erasers will work for this activity. Try erasers that are attached to pencils, small eraser tips that you use at the end of a pencil, or rectangular erasers. You may wish to try chalkboard erasers, depending on your students' skills. A child uses two erasers as tools for picking up other objects. He or she places one eraser in each hand. (The whole hand will need to be used for large erasers such as a chalkboard eraser. The child should use his or her index finger and thumb to hold smaller erasers.) The child grips an object between the two erasers and begins by moving an object such as a block from one location to another. As the child becomes skilled at moving an object, have him or her manipulate the object more. For example, he or she can place colored cubes or tiles in a pattern, move objects from a vertical position to a horizontal position, or arrange objects to form a circle.

Poking Activities

Pinhole Pictures

Create unique pictures with this technique using pushpins. Place an eraser tip on the end of the pushpin. This will make it easier to hold. Select a picture for this activity; a simple line drawing works well. Place the picture flat on the carpet or a carpet square. (A carpet with a short shag works best for this technique.) Demonstrate how to use a pin to poke a hole in the paper. A student pokes holes along the lines of the picture about every ½" (1.25 cm). **Teacher Note:** Be sure to discuss pin safety with the students before letting them participate in this task. When pictures are complete, hang them on a window to allow light to come through the pinholes. See pages 107–109 for some sample pictures. **Hint:** Golf tees and construction paper on carpet work well for younger children.

Pencil Poke Holes

Reproduce the cards on pages 110–112 onto cardstock. On the back of each card, circle the hole of the correct answer. Color the cards, then laminate for durability. Make the holes using a hole punch.

Have each child complete one poke hole card at a time. He or she should say the name of the picture quietly. The child pokes a finger, coffee stirrer, golf tee, or pencil tip in the hole that corresponds with the beginning sound of the picture. The child then looks at the back of the card to check his or her answer.

Create your own poke hole card by reproducing any simple pattern onto cardstock. Then punch 7–10 holes around the shape. Select a skill for review and add the appropriate details to the poke hole card.

Poking Activities *(cont.)*

Pinhole Patterns

Poking Activities (cont.)

Pinhole Patterns (cont.)

Poking Activities *(cont.)*

Pinhole Patterns *(cont.)*

Poking Activities (cont.)

Poke Hole Cards

H

D

K

G

W

L

Poking Activities *(cont.)*

Poke Hole Cards *(cont.)*

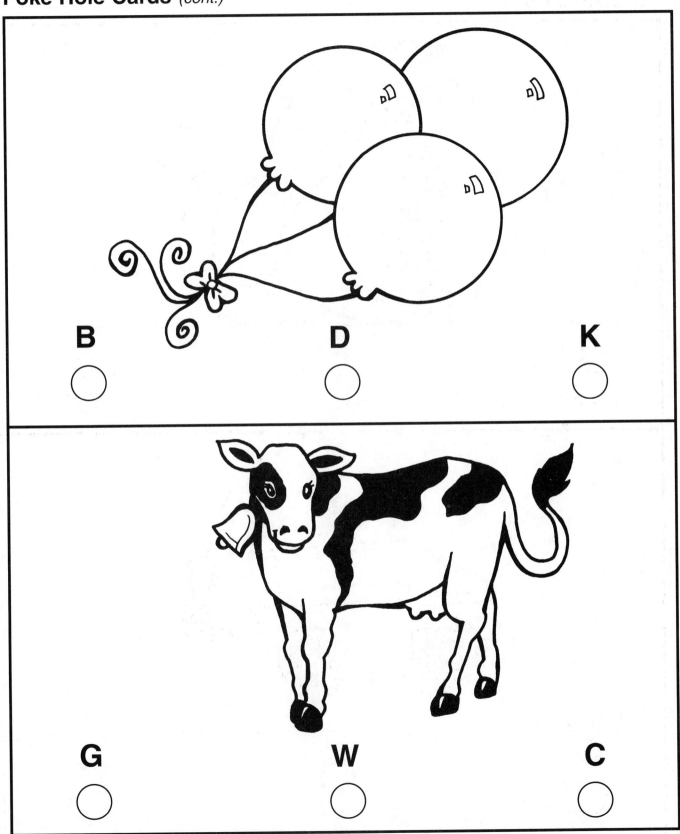

B

D

K

○

○

○

G

W

C

○

○

○

Poking Activities *(cont.)*

Poke Hole Cards *(cont.)*

F   **M**   **B**

Gluing Activities

Collage Pictures

Create your own collage bag. Fill a bag with scraps of material, tin foil, wrapping paper, ribbon, etc. Not only will your students have a great resource for art projects, but they will also be participating in recycling.

When the bag is ready, put some glue in a bowl or on a piece of wax paper for the children. To make an abstract collage, show each child how to select one item from the collage bag. Then demonstrate the following gluing technique. Dip one end of a cotton swab into the glue. Pick up the selected piece, rub the gluey end of the swab on it, and set the piece, glue-side down, onto heavy paper. Have each child randomly fill up his or her paper using this gluing technique. For older children, have them draw simple outline drawings first. Then direct each child to fill in the drawing by gluing down several collage pieces.

Pasta Pictures

On a tray, place glue and a bowl containing a variety of pastas. Cover the work area with newspaper. Locate simple pictures (a coloring book works well) for students to "color" with the pasta. Show each child how to stick the pasta shapes onto the paper. After the student has finished the picture, transfer it carefully to a cookie sheet to dry. (Remember not to pick up the picture quickly, or the pasta will fall off.) The picture can be displayed or framed when dry. You can also copy basic patterns, such as a tree or a turtle, on cardstock (or trace them onto cardboard). Have each student decorate the pattern in any design he or she wishes.

To make the pictures more interesting, place pasta in a brown paper bag. Drip several drops of food coloring into the bag; then close and shake the bag. Pour the colored pasta on a cookie sheet, covered with a paper towel, to dry before using. **Teacher Note:** Consider spray painting the completed patterns for your students with a solid color.

Gluing Activities *(cont.)*

Paper Chains

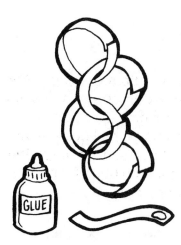

Paper chains make great decorations for holidays, and provide excellent fine motor practice. Vary the colors of construction paper to correspond with upcoming seasons or holidays (red and green for Christmas, blue and white for Hanukkah, pastels for spring). Gather a variety of colors of construction paper. Cut a large number of strips. Strips of paper that are 6" long and ½" wide (15 cm x 1.3 cm) work well for little hands. Show each student how to glue a paper chain strip together by placing a tiny drop of glue on the end of the strip and holding it tightly against the other end long enough for it to set. (Glue sticks also work well.) Help the student thread the second strip through the loop made by the first, before gluing it.

Tissue Paper Picture

Cut various colors of tissue paper into 1½" (3.84 cm) squares. Press the eraser end of a pencil on the center of one of the tissue paper squares. Use your fingers to bring the rest of the tissue paper around the pencil. Dip the end of the eraser in glue, then place the piece of tissue paper onto a sheet of paper. A student can create his or her own design or fill in the color on a picture. See pages 101–103 for simple patterns suitable for this activity.

Log Cabins

Place two craft sticks parallel to each other on a piece of cardboard. Glue them down lengthwise. Then place two more craft sticks opposite these but on top, so the ends of the new ones are on top of the ends of the first two, thereby creating a square. Put glue on top where the ends overlap. Stop when the log cabin is to the desired height. Fold a sheet of construction paper in half lengthwise; then open it up. Use the paper for the roof of the log cabin. For a yummy alternative to this activity, you may wish to use pretzels and icing.

Bean Frame

Provide a simple pattern for each student to use for this activity. (The patterns on pages 107–109 provide simple lines for students to follow.) He or she may color or paint the inside of the picture. The student then frames the picture by gluing beans around the dark outside edge of the pattern.

Games

Dominoes

Have each student create a domino maze by standing dominoes on one end in a line approximately 1" (2.5 cm) apart. He or she knocks the line down by tipping over the first domino in the line. Challenge the student to create curved lines or simple pictures with the dominoes.

Squirreling Objects

Spread out five beans on the table or floor in front of the children. Have each child pick up one bean with the pointer finger and thumb; then move the bean to the palm of the hand holding the bean in place with the remaining three fingers while picking up a second bean. The child moves the second bean to the palm of the hand (now he or she should be holding two beans). The child picks up a third bean and repeats the same action until all five beans have been picked up. Once all five beans have been picked up, have the child release the beans one at a time into an empty film canister or another container. Make this task more difficult by increasing the number of beans the child has to pick up. Use cereal, pennies, or beads in place of beans to vary the activity.

If using an object that comes in a variety of colors, require each student to drop the items in a patterned order. For example, if using red, yellow, and blue beads, have the student "squirrel" the objects in any order he or she wants. However, when dropping the beads, require that the red beads be released first, the yellow beads be released second, and the blue beads be released third. This will require the student to manipulate the objects in his or her hand in order to drop the beads in the correct order.

Penny Activities

Pennies are an easily accessible and inexpensive manipulative for fine motor activities. Gather approximately 25–30 pennies per student, and use some of the following activities to help develop students' finger coordination.

Penny Find

Pour uncooked, dry oats into a bowl or container. (The tall cylinder container that most oats come in works well for this activity; however, any type of container will work.) Place 20 pennies in the oats and shake the container firmly. Have students reach in the oats to fish out the hidden pennies. Other materials that work well for this activity include: dried rice, beans, macaroni, cornmeal, and Oobeleegook (see page 239).

Pennies in Water

Place 10 pennies in a container of water. The student reaches in the bucket to collect the pennies. It is not as easy as it sounds! Provide a cloth or paper towel for the student to dry the pennies once they have taken them out of the water.

Penny Wash

Have students wash pennies. Get a penny wet by dipping it into a small cup of vinegar. Then, place the wet penny in a small cup of salt. The salt will stick to the penny. Encourage each student to use his or her thumb and pointer finger to rub the pennies clean. Finally, he or she can rinse the penny with water. Have a penny wash near Lincoln's birthday; have a quarter wash near Washington's birthday.

Penny Activities *(cont.)*

Pennies in Play Dough

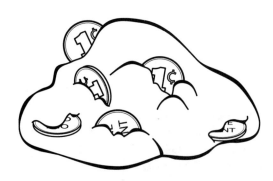

Each student will need a piece of play dough about the size of an adult fist. The play dough can be purchased or homemade (see the recipes on pages 233–237). Provide at least 10 pennies for each student. Encourage the student to press the pennies into the play dough with his or her fingers.

For a variation on this activity, hide the pennies in the play dough before giving it to a child. He or she searches through the play dough to find and pull out the pennies.

Pennies in the Round

Make a copy of the circle pattern on page 118. Have each child line the pennies heads-up on the outline of the circle. After the pennies make a complete circle, have the child turn the pennies over so that they are tail side-up. Have the child complete this activity with the pointer finger and thumb of his or her right hand, then left hand. Time each action to determine which one is faster.

Penny Patterns

Place red dot stickers on the heads side of at least 10 pennies per student. Place blue dot stickers on the tails side of those pennies. Have each student manipulate the red and blue pennies to create patterns. Begin with a simple AB pattern, such as red, blue, red, blue. As the student begins to demonstrate an understanding of AB patterns, show him or her how to make more complicated patterns such as ABB or AABB.

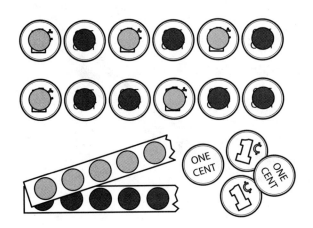

Penny Activities (cont.)

Pennies in the Round

Penny Activities *(cont.)*

Penny Stack

Have each student stack pennies one on top of the other. Begin by having the child create stacks with only two pennies in each.

As he or she demonstrates an ability to create two-penny stacks, have the student create taller stacks.

Have each student create several penny stacks. After the child has several stacks, encourage him or her to carefully pick up the penny stacks and place them one on top of the other. Then challenge the child to see how tall he or she can make stacks of pennies before they fall over.

Penny Trace

Gather appropriate writing tools (pencil, pen, or crayon) and paper. Have each child place a penny on the paper and trace around the outside edge of the penny with a pencil. In order to successfully trace around the penny, the child will have to use both hands. One hand holds the writing tool, and the other hand holds the penny in place. Encourage the child to use a pointer finger or thumb to hold the penny in place. If holding the penny is too difficult a task, stick the penny to the paper using tape or play dough. Doing this enables the child to focus on the task of tracing the penny. As he or she becomes more successful, increase the difficulty of the task by having the student hold the penny.

Penny Bag

Provide a stack of pennies for each student. Have the student place one penny in a resealable, plastic bag. Then, using his or her thumbs and index fingers, he or she seals the bag. The student picks up another penny, opens the bag, places the penny inside, and seals the bag again. He or she continues in this manner until all of the pennies are placed in the bag.

Penny Activities *(cont.)*

Squirreling Pennies

Spread at least five pennies on the table or floor. Have each child pick up one penny at a time using the pointer finger and thumb. A child moves the penny to the palm of the hand, holding the penny in place with the remaining three fingers while picking up a second penny. Then he or she moves the second penny to the palm of the hand (now the child should be holding two pennies). The child picks up a third penny. He or she repeats the action, moving the pennies to the palm of the hand until all five pennies have been picked up. Once all five pennies have been picked up, have the child release the pennies one at a time into an empty film canister, or other container, using the same hand. This is called "squirreling." Make this task more difficult by increasing the number of pennies the child has to pick up and hold.

Penny Balance

Have each student practice balancing a penny using only two fingers. He or she bends the pointer finger to form a crook. Then, the student places the thumb at a right angle touching the pointer finger. (The tip of the thumb should be touching the pad of the pointer finger.) After the student is able to successfully balance the penny, challenge him or her to a penny flick (see directions for Penny Flick).

Penny Flick

Place an empty shoe box about 12" (30 cm) from where the child is sitting. Have each child balance a penny on his or her pointer finger and thumb (see directions for Penny Balance). Using the thumb, he or she flicks the penny into the air aiming for the empty box. Then, the child repeats the action. (Challenge each child to flick 10 pennies into the box.) As the student becomes successful at completing this task, move the box farther away.

Penny Activities *(cont.)*

Piggy Bank

Provide a stack of pennies for each child. Have him or her pick up approximately 5–10 pennies. Holding the pennies in the palm of a closed hand, have the child manipulate his or her hands to push one penny at a time between the thumb and index finger. Then have the child drop each penny into a piggy bank. He or she repeats the action until all the pennies are in the piggy bank. If a piggy bank is not available, cut a slit in the top of a film container, margarine tub, or potato chip canister.

Penny Rotation

Have each child hold a penny between the thumb and index finger. He or she rotates the penny clockwise and then counterclockwise. Challenge the child to rotate two pennies, one in each hand, at the same time.

Penny Count

Fill each of 10 film containers with a set of pennies appropriate for your class. Number each lid with a number from 1–10. Complete an answer key and place it in an envelope. A student selects film container number 1, removes the lid, and counts the pennies in the container. Young students simply count the number of pennies in the container; older students can record the number of pennies in each container on the Penny Count Recording Sheet (page 123) in the appropriate space. The student can self-check his or her work using the answer key (see page 122). After returning the pennies to the container, the student continues to count the pennies in the remaining containers. (This activity makes a great center.)

Penny Activities *(cont.)*

Penny Count Answer Key

Complete an answer key and place it in an envelope. Create a new key each time you change the number of pennies in a container.

Penny Count Key			
Container	**Penny Count**	**Container**	**Penny Count**
#1		#1	
#2		#2	
#3		#3	
#4		#4	
#5		#5	
#6		#6	
#7		#7	
#8		#8	
#9		#9	
#10		#10	
Container	**Penny Count**	**Container**	**Penny Count**
#1		#1	
#2		#2	
#3		#3	
#4		#4	
#5		#5	
#6		#6	
#7		#7	
#8		#8	
#9		#9	
#10		#10	

Penny Activities *(cont.)*

Penny Count Recording Sheet

Directions: Take a container. Count the pennies. Record the number of pennies next to the container number.

Container	Penny Count
#1	
#2	
#3	
#4	
#5	
#6	
#7	
#8	
#9	
#10	

Clothespin Activities

Pinching a clothespin requires a student to coordinate his or her thumb and pointer finger in order to open and close it. The following activities provide that fine motor practice. Create a "Winged Clothespin" (see activity below) for a student who has difficulty using a regular clothespin.

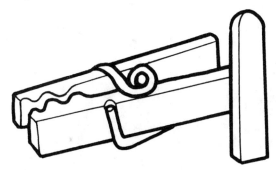

Matching Mittens

Create a clothesline. (See "Hanging Clothes" on this page for directions). Place a variety of pairs of mittens in a basket. Have a student look through the basket to find matching mitten pairs. When a pair is found, he or she hangs the pair on the clothesline using a clothespin.

If real mittens are not available, copy the patterns on pages 125 or 126. Color each pair using a matching pattern, and cut them out. (Enlarge the mitten patterns if desired.) A plain pair of mittens is provided on page 126. Create your own patterns on the plain mittens or have students create patterns on them. The mittens may be decorated with glue and glitter, or yarn.

Winged Clothespin

Cut a craft stick in half, and lightly sand the cut edges. Glue one-half of the craft stick perpendicular to the end of a wooden clothespin to make a winged clothespin. (See illustration.) A student uses a winged clothespin by placing a thumb on one side and his or her four fingers on the side with the half craft stick.

Hanging Clothes

Create a clothesline using two chairs and a piece of yarn. Tie each end of the yarn to a different chair; then pull the chairs apart so that the yarn is taut. Provide a basket of doll clothes (or baby clothes) and clothespins. Have each child pretend that he or she is washing the clothes. Then, the child uses the clothespins to hang up the clothes on the clothesline. If real clothes are not available, enlarge and copy the clothing patterns on pages 170–171 and cut off the tabs. Color and laminate the clothing patterns, then have students practice hanging them.

Clothespin Activities *(cont.)*

Mitten Patterns

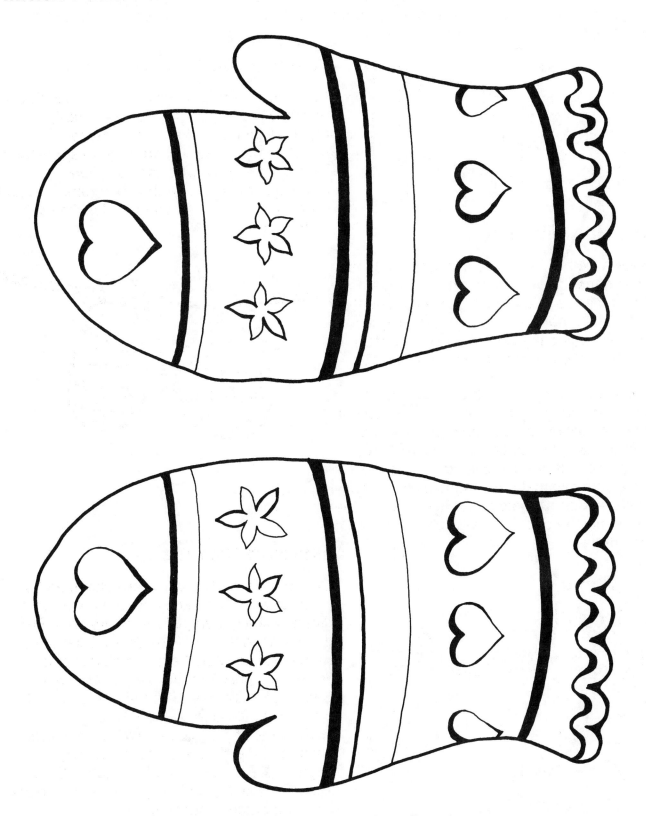

Clothespin Activities *(cont.)*

Mitten Patterns *(cont.)*

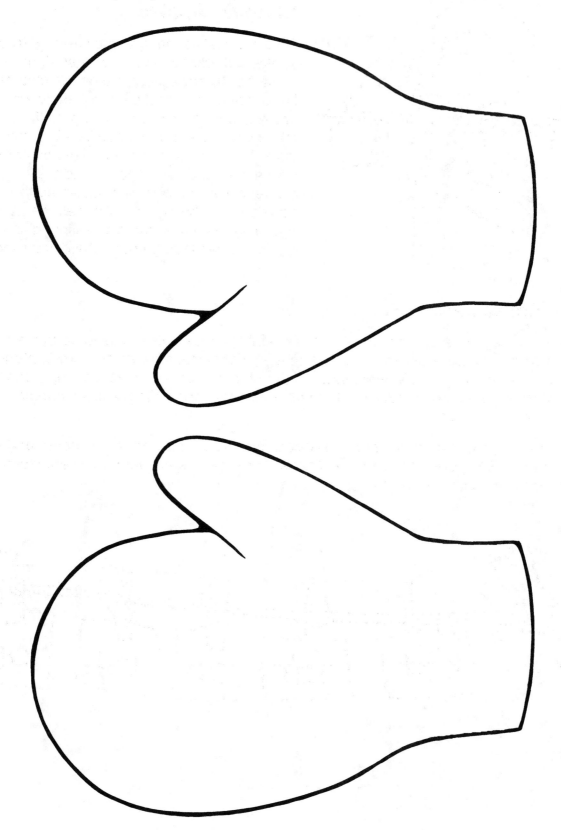

Clothespin Activities *(cont.)*

Hanging Apples

On a clothesline, hang approximately 10 paper apples with clothespins. Ask a student to count how many apples are on the clothesline. Have him or her practice taking down one apple at a time. While holding onto the apples taken down, the student continues to take down the remaining apples. Have him or her hold the apples in one hand, and the clothespin in the other without letting the apples fall to the ground. After all the apples have been taken off the clothesline, direct the student to reattach them on the clothesline.

Create a Sentence

Reproduce the word cards on pages 128–129. A student uses clothespins to hang the cards on a clothesline to create a sentence. Or have the student dictate his or her own sentence to you. Write the sentence on a sentence strip. He or she can cut the sentence strip apart so that each word, or punctuation mark, is on a separate card. The child practices hanging up the cards in the correct order.

This activity can be adapted to number sentences. Have students use the numbers and math symbols on page 130 to create number sentences. (You can create your own sentences using sentence strips or index cards.)

Clothespin Activities *(cont.)*

Word Cards

A	cat	sat	on
my	lap	.	?
Can	you	ride	play
a	bike	I	the

Clothespin Activities (cont.)

Word Cards (cont.)

like	_____	to
jump	dog	can
bark	.	see
sit	_____	.

Clothespin Activities *(cont.)*

Number Cards

0	1	2
3	4	5
6	7	8
9	+	−	=

Clothespin Activities *(cont.)*

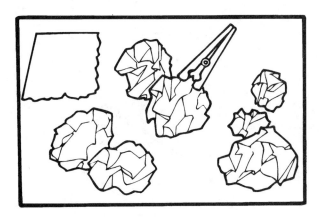

Crumple It

Provide each student with several sheets of paper. Recycled or used paper works well. Have the student use his or her hands to crumple up the paper into a ball. (See if the student can perform this action using only one hand.) Then, scatter the crumpled balls of paper on the floor. Have the student use a clothespin to pick up the balls of paper, and throw them into a box or trash can.

Clothespin Games

Reproduce the clothespin games onto cardstock. (See pages 132–136 for clothespin game patterns.) Color the cards and write the answers on the back for self-checking. Laminate the cards for durability. Referring to the directions at the bottom of each game, write the corresponding words on the clothespins.

Each student takes one card and the labeled clothespins that go with it. Have him or her look at the word or number on each clothespin, then clip the clothespin to its match on the card. The student self-checks his or her answer by flipping the card over. You may wish to store the game card and the clothespins together in a large resealable, plastic bag.

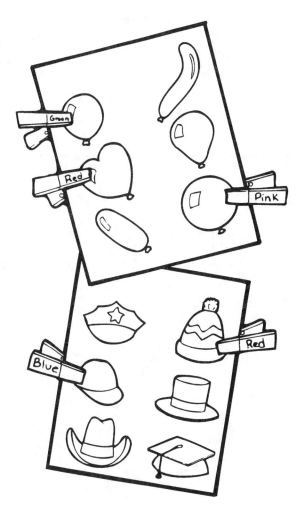

Clothespin Activities *(cont.)*

Balloon Clothespin Game

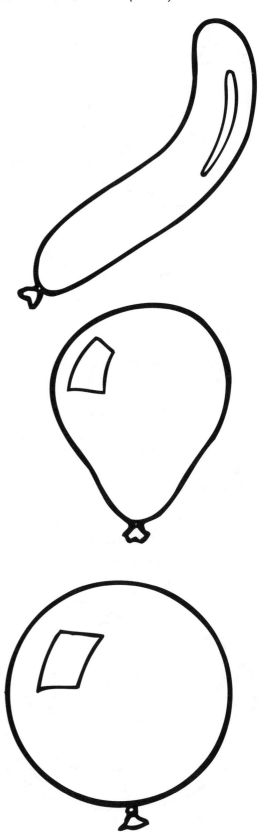

✂ -

Directions: Color each balloon a different color. For each balloon, program (label) one clothespin with the name of its color.

Clothespin Activities *(cont.)*

Hat Clothespin Game

✄---

Directions: Color each hat a different color. For each hat, program (label) one clothespin with the name of its color.

Clothespin Activities *(cont.)*

Number Clothespin Game

✂--

Directions: Program (label) each clothespin with a number from 1–10.

Clothespin Activities *(cont.)*

Letter Clothespin Game

d

n

k

w

a

j

t

h

l

q

✂--

Teacher Note: Program (label) each clothespin with a corresponding uppercase letter.

Clothespin Activities *(cont.)*

Letter Clothespin Game *(cont.)*

A   G

F   I

R   H

Y   M

B   E

✂--

Teacher Note: Program (label) each clothespin with a corresponding lowercase letter.

Clothespin Activities *(cont.)*

Clothespin Pick-Up

Begin by spreading objects on the table or floor. Have each student use a clothespin to pick up objects and move them to a desired location. For example, you may spread cotton balls on the table. Require that the student pick up five cotton balls with a clothespin (one at a time) and return them to a bowl.

Turn this activity into a relay race. A student holds a clothespin in each hand, then grabs a cotton ball in each clothespin. The student hops, jumps, or walks to a container at the opposite side of the room where he or she releases the objects held by clothespins into the container.

Clothespin Drop

Place an empty one-gallon milk carton on the floor. (If desired, use a container with a larger opening for younger students.) A student stands with his or her feet touching the milk carton. Have him or her hold a clothespin between the thumb and pointer finger. He or she tries to drop the clothespin into the milk carton. In addition, a student can pick up an item (such as an eraser) with the clothespin and try to drop the object in the container.

Punctuation Clips

Reproduce the sentence strips on pages 138–139 onto cardstock. Mark clothespins with periods, question marks, and exclamation points. On the back of each strip, write the correct punctuation mark so that a student can self-check his or her work. You may wish to store the pieces for this activity in a resealable, plastic bag.

A child lays all the sentence strips on the floor. He or she reads each strip quietly and decides if the sentence is a telling sentence, asking sentence, or exciting sentence. If it is a telling sentence, he or she clips a clothespin with a period to the end of the sentence strip. If it is an asking sentence, the child clips a clothespin with a question mark to the end of the sentence. If a sentence shows excitement, he or she clips a clothespin with an exclamation point to the end of the sentence strip. After attaching a clothespin to each sentence, the child turns over each strip to check work.

Clothespin Activities (cont.)

Punctuation Sentence Strips

What is the puppy's name

How old are you

He hit the winning home run

Where do you live

Did you like the movie

Clothespin Activities (cont.)

Punctuation Sentence Strips (cont.)

The little girl likes to jump rope	That house is on fire	They like to ride their bikes	The birthday party was fun	Please put on your coat

Using Scissors .

The idea of controlling an object to make cuts is a fascinating one. You usually will not have a difficult time persuading children to use scissors. Children undoubtedly will have seen adults using scissors, and often have a desire to learn how to use them.

When introducing scissors, remember to discuss safety with the children. Remind them that children only use scissors for cutting objects when an adult gives them permission. You may also want to give some directions about properly and safely handling scissors.

In addition, you will want to provide some instruction regarding correct ways of holding scissors. Determine a student's hand dominance, if appropriate. The student's thumb will go in one hole and the middle finger goes in the other hole. The ring and little finger should be bent in the palm for stability. (If a student has a difficult time keeping fingers bent, have him or her hold an eraser or wadded-up piece of paper in the ring and little finger while holding the scissors.)

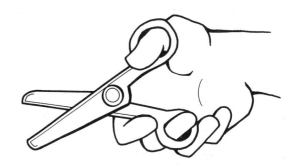

When cutting, the thumb should be pointed up toward the ceiling. The elbow and arm (of the hand holding the scissors) should be held in toward the body. The hand holding the paper is the same hand (and arm) that moves and rotates the paper.

Scissors activities are provided on the following pages. The activities are listed in sequential order, following a progression of cutting skills.

Teacher Note: Have plenty of supervision if you are introducing scissors for the first time to a large group of children. It is preferable to do this in small groups. Be sure to provide plenty of time for children to experiment with the scissors the first time they are allowed to handle them.

Progression of Cutting Skills

In assessing a child's cutting skills, refer to the following outline. It shows a typical progression of cutting skills.

Pre-Scissors Activities: A student needs to have the strength and coordination in order to squeeze and release before he or she can use scissors. Activities involving the squeeze and release motion can be found on page 142.

Tearing: This involves pulling hands away from the middle to tear the paper (reciprocal), or one hand coming toward the body and the other hand pulling away (bilateral).

Snipping: The width of paper is about two-thirds of the scissors' blades.

Fringing: The width of the paper is 1" (2.5 cm) longer than the scissors' blades.

Strips: The paper is 6–8" (15– 20 cm) long and 4–6" (10–15 cm) wide.

Angles: The child cuts and then stops in the middle of the paper, turning the paper and cutting again.

Rounded Shapes: The child turns and cuts the paper at the same time.

Curves: The child turns the paper and cuts until he or she returns to where the cutting began.

Spirals: The child cuts a spiral, working from the outside to the inside.

Simple Figure Shapes: The child cuts one line that makes a simple figure (e.g., a heart, an outline of a duck, etc.)

Complex Figure Shapes: With multiple lines on the page, the child determines which lines to cut in order to cut the outline of the figure (e.g., a picture of a clown).

       #3689 Activities for Fine Motor Skills Development

Progression of Cutting Skills *(cont.)*

Finger Touches

Have each student practice touching the pad of the thumb to the pads of the other fingers (on the same hand). The student begins with an open hand. Then, he or she touches the pad of the thumb to the pad of the pinkie finger, and opens the hand again. Next, the student touches the pad of the thumb to the pad of the ring finger, and opens the hand again. He or she continues until the thumb has touched all fingers. To add fun to this activity, place a small round sticker on the pad of each finger.

Have each student practice closing the hand by touching the pad of the thumb to the pad of both the index finger and the middle finger at the same time. (The ring and pinkie finger are bent into the palm and do not move.) This is the same motion required to open and close the scissors.

Open/Close

Once you provide children with scissors, give them some time to practice coordinating their fingers to open/close the scissors. Have them open and close the scissors without trying to cut anything yet, just the air!

Hanging String

Tape a piece of string from a table edge so that the string hangs down. A student practices cutting the string by making only one open/close movement with the scissors. At the bottom of the hanging string, he or she begins cutting it shorter and shorter as more cuts are made. Use a variety of colors of string. The cut-up string can be used to fill in the color on mosaic pictures such as those found on pages 145–148. Or, use the string as the hair on the paper bears found on pages 170–171.

Play Dough

An excellent way to develop the open/close coordination required to cut is to provide each student with a lump of play dough. (See recipes on pages 233–237.) Encourage him or her to practice the open/close movement by cutting the play dough lump.

Roll the play dough into "snakes" and have students practice cutting the "snakes." You can hold the "snake" in the air for the student. Or, if you have a surface that will not get scratched, a student can practice cutting the "snakes" on the tabletop. (An old cookie tray or cutting board makes a good tabletop surface to practice cutting.) As a student becomes skilled at cutting the "snakes," have him or her hold the "snake" in preparation for holding paper.

Art Activities

Wreaths

Cut a circle from the center of a paper plate to form a wreath. A student tears green tissue paper into small pieces, then glues the tissue paper onto the paper-plate rim until it is covered. He or she punches a hole in the top and laces yarn through the hole for hanging the wreath. **Note:** The student may add sequins and other decorations using tweezers.

Paint Chips

Obtain paint chip samples from your local paint store. Have each child practice cutting the paint chip apart by making snips. A child should be able to make one snip in order to cut the paint chip into two pieces. To begin with, he or she can practice cutting anywhere on the paint chip. As the student becomes more skilled at using scissors, have him or her try to cut "on the lines," cutting the various shades apart. Once a student has cut apart a paint chip, have him or her take one color from the paint chip and walk around the room to find something else that matches the color on the paint chip.

Grocery Store Collage

Have the children cut out pictures of food and other items from grocery store ads. Cut large brown paper bags into various sizes. Let each child choose his or her own sack and glue pictures onto it to create a grocery store collage.

Art Activities *(cont.)*

Mosaic Tear Art

Demonstrate for students how to tear a sheet of paper into small pieces. Provide a variety of colors for students to practice tearing. When torn, pieces should be about the size of a quarter or smaller. Have students sort the paper by color and store the pieces in containers (empty margarine containers work well). When enough pieces of each color are ready, have each student create a collage picture by gluing pieces onto a mosaic pattern. (See pages 145–148 for pattern ideas.)

Decorated Bottle

Provide a variety of colors of tissue paper. Students tear the tissue paper into small pieces. Find a small bottle or empty jar to decorate. Create a mixture of half liquid starch and half water. A student places a piece of tissue paper on the bottle. He or she uses a paintbrush dipped in the starch mixture, and paints over the piece of tissue paper to hold it in place. When the glue/starch dries, the tissue paper will be stuck to the bottle, creating a shiny surface. For more practice and extra shine, add a top coat of the starch mixture.

Mosaic Pictures

Once students learn how to control the scissors a little better, you will probably find that they want to use scissors all the time! Excellent practice for students is to cut paper. When students are able to cut pieces about the size of a quarter, encourage them to combine cutting and gluing skills to make a mosaic picture. Provide students with a variety of colors of construction paper with which to practice cutting little pieces. Each student takes the pieces he or she cuts and glues them onto a pattern to fill in the color for the picture. Mosaic picture patterns are provided on pages 145–148. Coloring books with large shapes also provide excellent patterns to use for mosaics.

Art Activities *(cont.)*

Mosaic Picture Patterns

Art Activities *(cont.)*

Mosaic Picture Patterns *(cont.)*

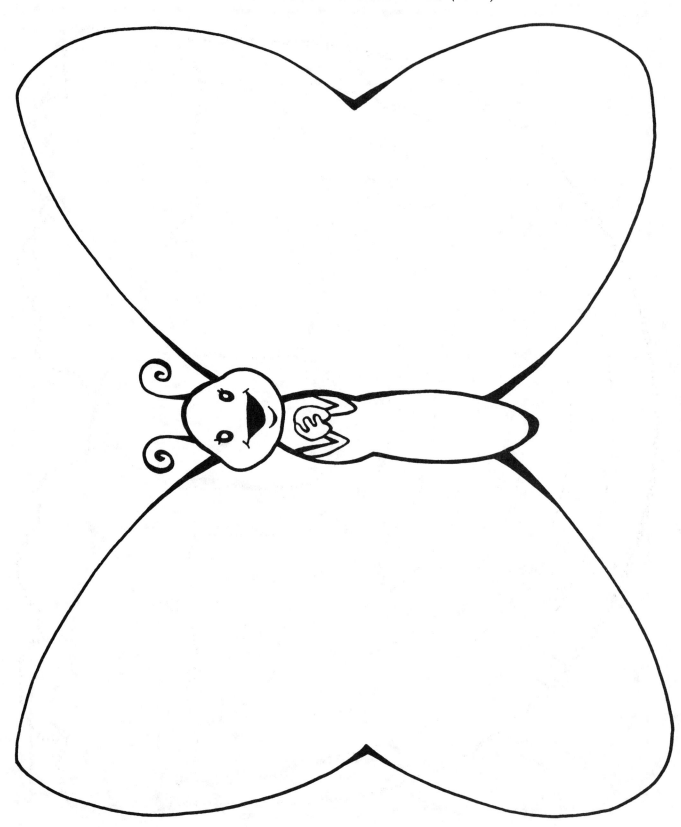

Art Activities (cont.)

Mosaic Picture Patterns (cont.)

Art Activities (cont.)

Mosaic Picture Patterns (cont.)

Patterning Activities

Straws

Each student can practice taking one cut by cutting a drinking straw. First, he or she cuts the straw in half, then into smaller pieces. Provide play dough for the students to poke the straws into (once they have cut all of the straws into smaller pieces). Encourage each student to create a pattern as he or she pokes the straws into the play dough. For example, a student can create a pattern of tall straw, short straw, tall straw, short straw. Use a variety of colors of straws so that each student can create a color pattern.

The cut-up straw pieces can be used to create a necklace. Wrap tape around the tip of a piece of yarn or string to form a "needle" tip. A student holds the string in one hand and guides the pieces of straw on the string with the other hand. Encourage the student to create patterns on his or her necklace (if straws of different colors are used).

Paper Strips

Cut strips of paper to approximately ½ the size of the scissors' blades and have students practice cutting this size of paper. If it is accessible, use cardstock. Postcards or advertisements that are printed on heavier paper are also excellent materials for cutting practice. Each student should be able to cut the paper in half with only one cut or one open/close movement. As a student becomes more skilled at cutting paper with one cut, make the strips of paper a little wider until the student has to make two cuts to cut the paper in half. Continue making the paper strips wider as the student becomes skilled.

Save all of the scrap paper that students have cut. When enough scraps have been saved, enlist your students' help in sorting the paper by color. Create a wall mural by copying one of the patterns on pages 145–148 onto transparency paper. Lay the transparency on an overhead projector and project the image onto a piece of butcher paper that has been hung on the wall. Trace each of the lines projected on the paper to draw the image. Have students use the scrap paper to fill in the color on the wall mural. Students glue the paper inside the line drawing of the mural.

Fringes

Begin with strips of paper 3" (8 cm) wide. A child does not cut through the paper completely, but only makes one open/close movement to cut the paper. After the cut has been made, have the child move his or her scissors over 1" (2.5 cm) or so and make another cut. He or she continues until the end of the paper is reached. The effect is a fringed paper that resembles grass. As the student becomes more skilled at fringing paper, increase the width of the paper so that he or she will have to make more open/close movements with the scissors.

Have each child cut fringes on green paper to be used for grass on a picture. Have the child draw a picture of an outdoor scene. When the picture is complete, have him or her glue fringed green paper at the bottom of the picture for the grass.

When a child is able to make about three cuts with the scissors to fringe the paper, show him or her how to vary the number of cuts to fringe the paper in a pattern. For example, the first cut on the paper should have the length of just one cut. Next the child makes two cuts, and finally, the child makes three cuts. He or she continues by repeating the pattern.

Cutting Practice

Rounding up Business Cards

Collect or save business cards; they provide a firm paper that is excellent for students to practice cutting. Students can practice cutting the business cards in half. As students become skilled in cutting straight lines, encourage them to cut curved lines. An excellent way to begin doing this is to have them cut the corners off the business cards. At first, the cuts can be straight lines. Then, show each student how to turn the cards in order to make a curved line. When he or she becomes skilled at rounding the corners, the shape of the business card becomes almost oval. Save the rounded business cards for students to use as stencils. Each student can practice tracing around the business card as additional practice controlling a pencil.

Dots

Randomly glue or color dots on a sheet of paper. A student cuts from the edge of the paper until he or she reaches a dot, then cuts to another dot. The more dots on the paper, the more difficult the activity.

More Practice

Consider using some of the following materials for additional cutting practice: magazines, sales ads, junk mail, envelopes, sand paper, tissue paper, grocery store bags, wax paper, index cards, wallpaper samples, and old phone books. Pages 151–171 are specifically designed for cutting practice once a student is skilled with the open/close movement of the scissors.

Combine cutting activities with other skills or concepts the students are working on. Label a piece of chart paper or tagboard with a title. Have students search for and cut out pictures that illustrate the chosen concept. Glue the pictures to the chart after students have cut them out. Some topics might include:

- Letters
- Numbers
- Shapes
- Colors
- More/Less
- Large/Small
- Directions (over, under)
- Things that make sounds
- Longer/Shorter

Cutting Practice *(cont.)*

Directions: Practice cutting along each line.

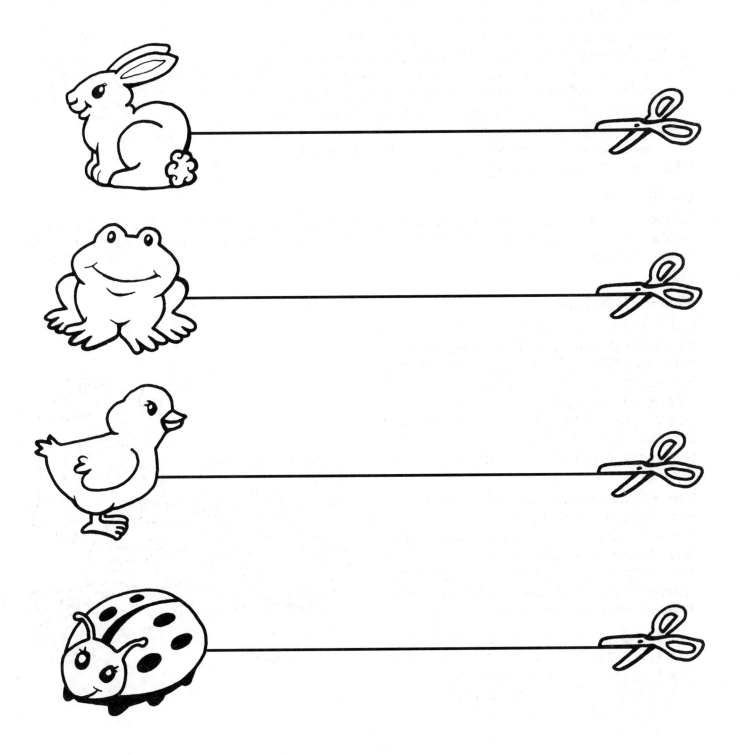

Cutting Practice *(cont.)*

Directions: Practice cutting along each line. Cut along the angled lines by stopping at each point and changing directions.

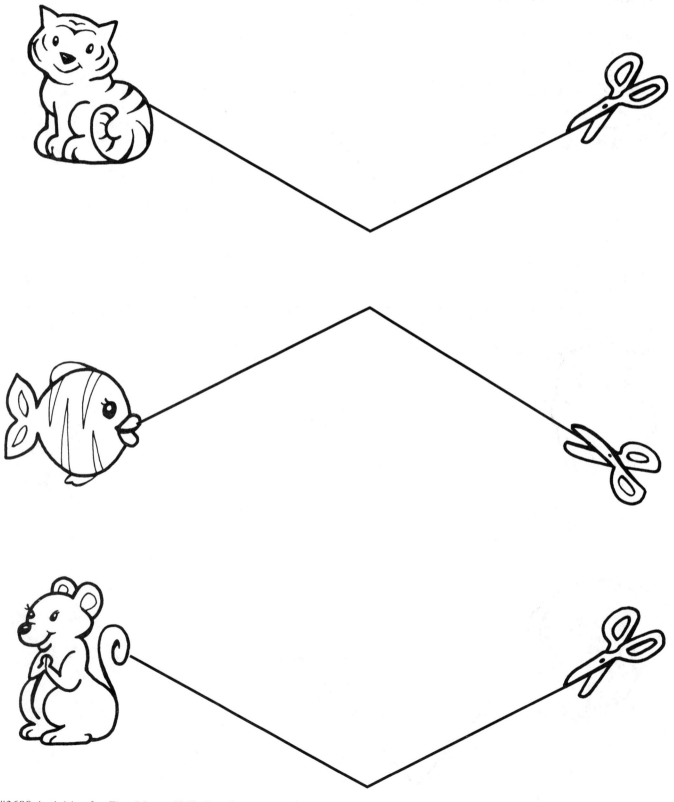

Cutting Practice *(cont.)*

Directions: Practice cutting along each line. Cut along the angled lines by stopping at each point and changing directions.

Cutting Practice *(cont.)*

Directions: Practice cutting along each line. Cut with one hand while turning the paper with the other.

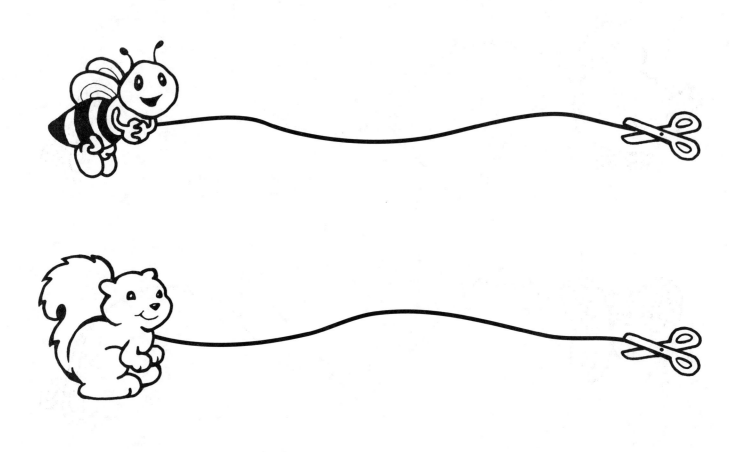

Cutting Practice *(cont.)*

Directions: Practice cutting along each line. Cut with one hand while turning the paper with the other.

Cutting Practice *(cont.)*

Sammy Snake

Directions: Color Sammy Snake. Cut out Sammy Snake. Make Sammy Snake by cutting on the dotted line. Begin at the tail. For fun, tie a string on the end of your snake, so that you can hang it up.

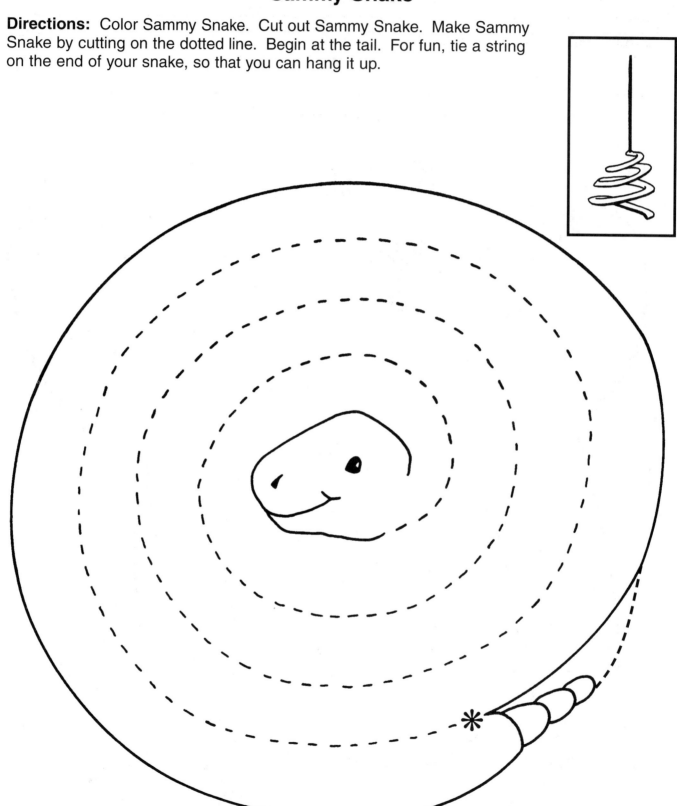

Cutting Practice *(cont.)*

Spooky Ghost

Directions: Cut out the ghost. Make the spooky ghost by cutting on the dotted line. Start at the star. For fun, tie a string on the end of your ghost so that you can hang it up.

Cutting Practice *(cont.)*

Roll of the Dice

Directions: Cut out the squares below. Glue them on the dice.

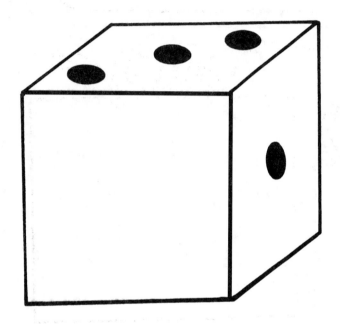 

 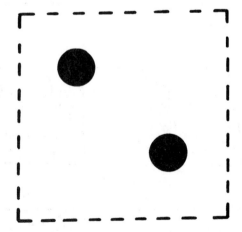

Cutting Practice *(cont.)*

What's Inside?

Directions: Cut out the wrapping paper designs below. Glue each design onto the correct gift. Cut on dashed lines only.

Cutting Practice *(cont.)*

Pizza, Pizza

Directions: Cut out the slices of pizza below. Glue each slice on a triangle on the pie pan.

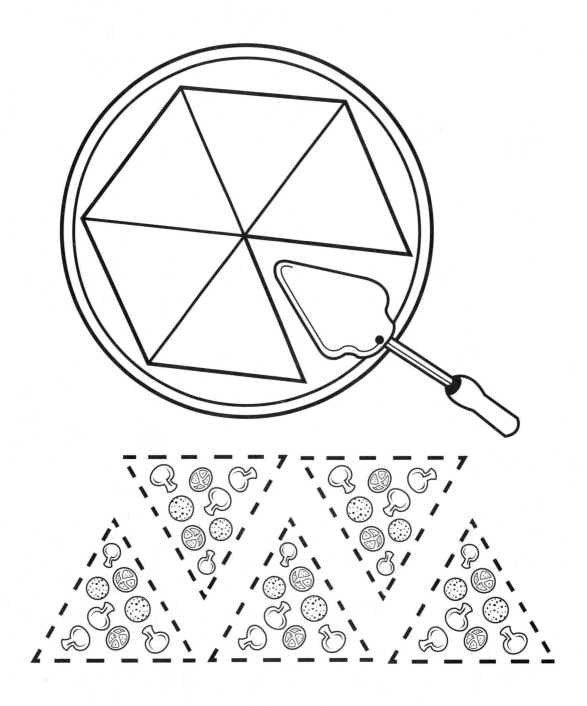

Cutting Practice *(cont.)*

Seeing Spots

Directions: Cut out the kittens. Glue each kitten in order from the one with the least number of spots to the most.

Cutting Practice *(cont.)*

Butterfly Wings

Directions: Cut out the butterfly wings. Match a pair of wings. Glue each pair onto a butterfly.

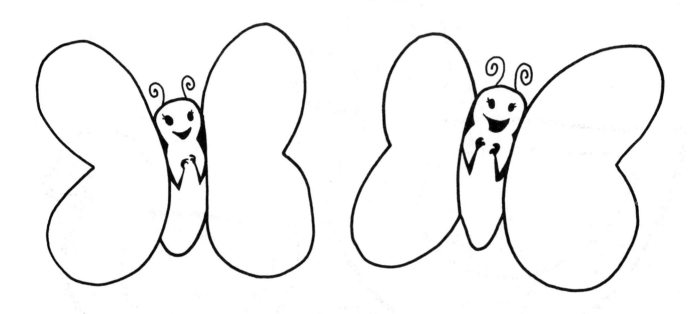

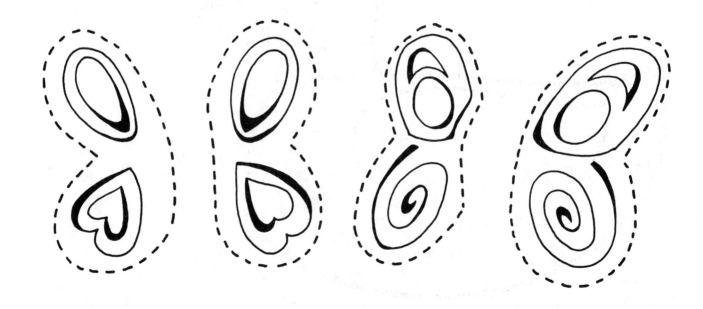

Cutting Practice *(cont.)*

Directions: Practice cutting along the outline of each shape. Cut with one hand while turning the paper with the other. Glue the ducks onto a piece of paper and add details to create a scene.

Cutting Practice *(cont.)*

Directions: Practice cutting along the outline of each shape. Cut with one hand while turning the paper with the other. Glue the fish onto a piece of light blue paper. Add details.

Cutting Practice *(cont.)*

Directions: Cut out the shapes below. Glue them in the blank box to make a flower like
the one above. Add your own details. Color both flowers.

My Flower

Cutting Practice *(cont.)*

A Face

Directions: Color and cut out your favorite face pieces on page 167 (two eyes, two ears, a mouth, and a nose). Use them to make a face on the head pattern. Glue the face pieces in place.

Cutting Practice (cont.)

A Face (cont.)

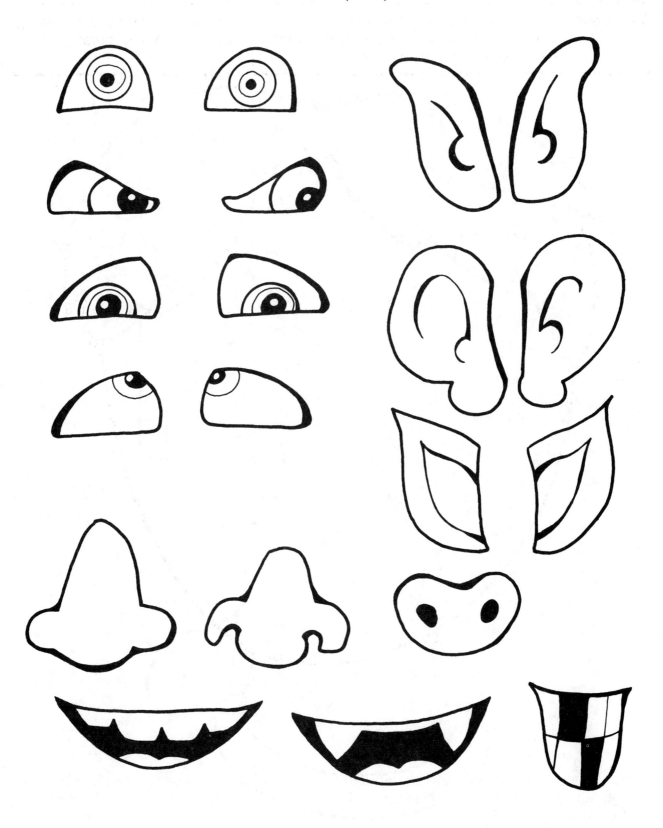

Cutting Practice *(cont.)*

Complex Shapes

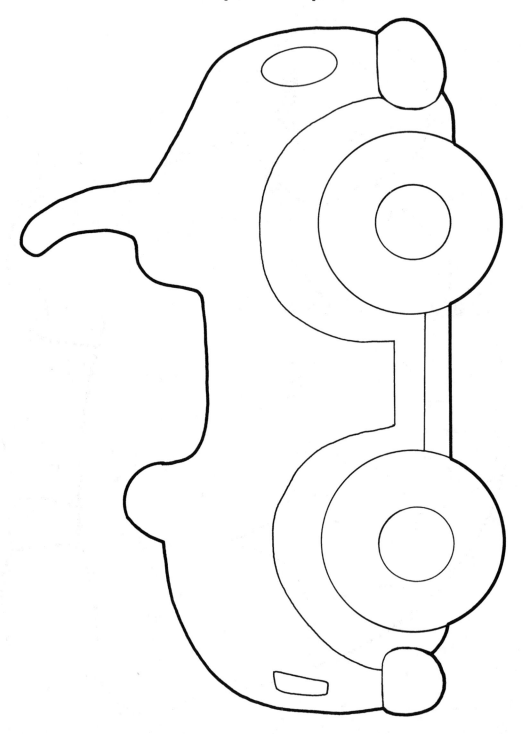

✂ -

Teacher Note: When introducing students to more complex drawings with multiple lines on the page, it is useful to use a highlighter or crayon to highlight the lines that the students will be cutting out.

Cutting Practice (cont.)

Complex Shapes (cont.)

✂ -

Teacher Note: When introducing students to more complex drawings with multiple lines on the page, it is useful to use a highlighter or crayon to highlight the lines that the students will be cutting out.

Cutting Practice *(cont.)*

Paper Bears

Encourage scissors practice by having each student cut out paper bears and clothing patterns. In order to play with the paper bears, a student manipulates his or her thumbs and index fingers to dress the dolls, providing additional fine motor skill practice. (Enlarge these patterns as needed.) Then, he or she can select a favorite outfit for each bear and glue it on.

Cutting Practice *(cont.)*

Paper Bears *(cont.)*

Drawing and Writing Guidelines

This section provides a variety of activities for both drawing and writing. Very young children can explore, while children who are ready can begin to make shapes, letters, numbers, or even words. The following are some guidelines for drawing and writing development.

Drawing

In assessing children's fine motor skills in regards to drawing, refer to these guidelines:

- 1–2 years: random scribbling
- 2–2½ years: controlled scribbling
- 2½–3 years: beginning to make faces
- 3½–4 years: adding stick arms and legs to the face
- 4 years: adding a body to the head, arms, and legs
- 5 years: adding houses that generally "float" on the page
- 5½–6 years: resting house on the paper's edge

Pre-Writing

In assessing children's fine motor skills in regards to pre-writing, refer to the guidelines below that show the progression of pre-writing skills:

- The child uses his or her fist to hold a crayon and makes incidental marks.
- The child imitates scribbles.
- The child makes purposeful marks.
- The child holds a writing tool with his or her fingers (incorrectly, but not fisted).
- The child draws a ball.
- The child traces a vertical line.
- The child traces a horizontal line.
- The child uses the correct grasp on a writing tool (by age 5).

Tactile Activities

The activities below and on pages 174–180 are ideal for students who have not yet begun writing with a pencil, or for students to practice making shapes, letters, or numbers. Students can use their fingers to explore writing in different textures.

Sand Writing

Provide children with a tray filled halfway with sand. (Use a brightly-colored tray if possible for contrast. For variety, use dry coffee grounds, salt, rice, or flour in place of sand.) Demonstrate how to "write" in the sand with your index finger. Be sure to let each child lead and make marks and shapes for you to copy, too. Also, you may wish to use a large sand tray for this activity so that the child can practice making more than one letter or symbol at a time.

Bag of Paint

Fill several half-gallon resealable, plastic bags with 2–3 tablespoons (30–45 mL) of paint. Seal tightly. Younger children can explore, while older children can practice writing. Prepare a large chart of the symbols, letters, numbers, or words you would like the children to practice. Lay the bag of paint on a flat surface. Each child uses his or her hands to smooth out the paint in the bag. The child uses his or her fingers to practice writing on top of the bag.

It helps to have several bags made up ahead of time in case a bag gets torn. Then it can be thrown away and another is readily available. For a variation on this activity, use a bag of pudding or hair gel.

Tactile Activities *(cont.)*

Shaving Cream

Provide cookie sheets or pizza pans and a can of shaving cream. Each student sprays enough shaving cream to cover the palm of his or her hand, then wipes the hand over the pizza pan to cover it. Using an index finger, he or she can practice drawing and writing.

For a twist, sprinkle powdered tempera paint over the shaving cream. Let the children mix in the color as they create with the shaving cream. Try this same activity with whipping cream, pudding, or colored bath foam.

Teacher Note: Caution children not to put shaving cream in their mouths or eyes.

Finger Paint

Clear a workspace that has a comfortable place for children to sit. You may want to do this activity outdoors. Cover the work area with a thick pad of newspaper to help soak up the water. Pour, or spoon, finger paint (see page 238 for finger paint recipes) into paper cups or containers. Make available just one or two colors for painting. Too many colors may produce a muddy-looking result. If you are using poster paint, mix it with some liquid laundry starch.

Place finger-paint paper on the work surface. Wet the paper with a sponge to keep the paper from flying away, and to make it easier to spread the paint. Show each child how to make different designs or simple shapes, using the side of the hand as well as the fingers. As pictures are completed, you can use clothespins to pin them up to dry.

Teacher Note: Try using a variety of types of paper, including paper plates when finger painting.

Pudding

Make some instant pudding following the package directions. Give each child a piece of wax paper and a few spoonfuls of the pudding. Give the child some time to paint on the wax paper with the pudding. Pudding can be used in place of the paint in half-gallon, resealable plastic bags. (See page 173 for directions on how to assemble a bag.)

Art Activities

There are many drawing and coloring activities that can be done with writing tools. Students become familiar with holding and using writing tools through drawing and coloring activities.

Introduce drawing and coloring activities to your students by using short broken crayons or disk crayons. As students become skilled with writing with broken crayons, introduce them to other types of writing tools, such as pencils, chalk, colored pencils, and even pens or markers.

Crayon Disks

Crayon disks are simply crayons which a student can hold with his or her whole hand instead of having to grip a crayon with only fingers. Making crayon disks is a great way to sort and use old and broken crayons, as well as making new, useful writing/coloring tools for your students. Spray an old muffin pan with cooking spray. Place several broken, similarly-colored crayons in the compartments of the muffin pan (be sure to remove the paper labels). You will want to have each compartment of the muffin pan filled about half way. Place the muffin pan in the oven at 350° F (180° C) and allow the crayons to melt (about 15 minutes). Keep an eye on the crayons as they melt; they may need to be removed from the oven earlier. After the wax cools and hardens, remove the new disk crayons from the muffin pan compartments. Use the new crayon disks to write or draw pictures. To make a multicolored disk, melt two or three different colored crayons together. (Mixing too many colors or too many dark colors will result in a muddy color.)

Stained Glass Crayon Art

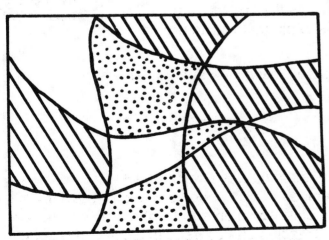

Have each student use a black crayon to create a variety of curved lines on a sheet of white paper. Then, he or she uses various colors to fill in the spaces created by the lines. For a challenge, have the student complete this task using as few colors as possible without having the same colors touch. This activity can be done using paint and a paintbrush. For additional practice tracing lines, have a student trace over the lines on the pattern on page 176.

Art Activities *(cont.)*

Stained Glass Crayon Art

Art Activities *(cont.)*

Chalk Drawing

Have each child create a drawing with chalk on a sheet of blue construction paper. A nice idea for this project is to draw a snowman. He or she gives the snowman eyes, a nose, mouth, hat, arms, scarf, and buttons. Have each child use a small red paper mitten to glue on the snowman as his heart.

Plastic Patterns

Place a piece of plastic, such as a lid to a coffee can or a plastic placemat, over one of the patterns on pages 178–179. Trace the pattern onto the plastic with a permanent marker. Using a craft knife or scissors, cut the shape out. Place the plastic pattern under a sheet of white paper. Have each student rub a crayon (with the paper peeled off) horizontally over the paper where the pattern is. He or she will see the pattern appear on the paper. Disk crayons work well for this activity; however, any crayon will work. Each student can use his or her patterns to create a whole scene, adding details holding crayons in the traditional manner. For example, once the dinosaur pattern has been traced onto a sheet of paper, the student can add trees, volcanoes, clouds, and other animals.

Leaf Rubbings

Collect as many types of fresh, fallen leaves as possible. Tape one down on a table surface for a student to create a rubbing. Have him or her put a piece of newsprint over it. The student uses a side of a peeled crayon or pieces of chalk to rub gently over the leaf several times until the image of a leaf appears. Then the child compares the rubbing he or she made with others to determine whether the same type of leaf was used. Have the child dictate a sentence to you about fall, his or her leaf, or collecting leaves. Try rubbings with a variety of materials such as: keys, coins, paper clips, rubber bands, etc.

Art Activities *(cont.)*

Plastic Patterns

Art Activities *(cont.)*

Plastic Patterns *(cont.)*

Art Activities *(cont.)*

Line Drawing

With a black marker, make straight or curved lines on sheets of white paper. A student selects a sheet to make into a picture. Have him or her study the black line on the page. Tell the student to turn the paper horizontally or vertically, depending on what he or she plans to create from the line. Encourage the student to use creativity in making the line into a picture. Have him or her color the picture and make up a story to go with it.

Half Pictures

Locate a variety of simple pictures (from magazines or from the patterns on pages 145–148). Cut the pictures in half. A student glues the "half picture" to a sheet of paper. Then, he or she uses a crayon to complete the other half of the picture.

Magic Pictures

Create magic pictures that will be invisible at first, but visible later. Have each child use lemon juice on cotton swabs to paint a picture on a sheet of white paper. When finished, emphasize that only an adult can do the part to make the picture show. Hold the paper a few inches above a shining light bulb. The child will be amazed to see his or her magic picture. He or she may want to send the mystery magic picture, along with instructions for decoding it, to a relative or friend.

Writing Activities

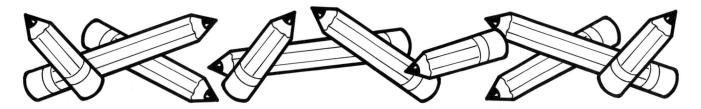

A correct pencil grip will help a student in everything from drawing basic shapes to printing, to even handwriting. Introducing a correct pencil grip to your students by demonstrating it may be the only instruction some students will need; however, many students need repeated practice and demonstrations of an acceptable position for the fingers when holding and using a pencil (or other writing tool).

Pencil Grip

An acceptable pencil grip is any grip on the pencil in which a circle is formed by the thumb and index finger, once the fingers are holding the pencil. After the fingers have been placed on the pencil, they should be able to freely move the pencil. Typically, the thumb and index finger are opposite each other. The thumb is on the bottom and the index finger is on the top of the pencil. The middle finger usually supports the pencil, while the ring finger and the little finger are bent and resting in the palm. However, there are other positions that the middle finger, ring finger, and little finger can be in that will still yield an acceptable pencil grip.

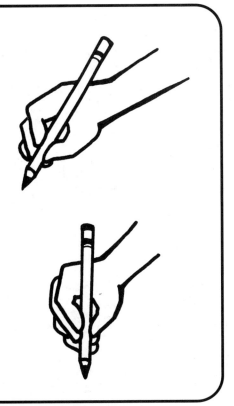

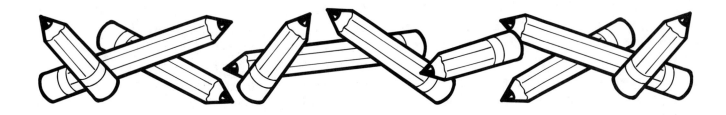

Pencil Grip Activities

Media Variety

Allow students to use and experiment with a variety of writing media. Let each student experiment with his or her fingers by writing in shaving cream, sand, paint, finger paint, rice, and pudding. Provide a variety of writing tools including: gel pens, chalk, crayons, colored pencils, pens, crayon disks, #2 pencils, #1 pencils, markers, and felt-tipped pens.

Nail Polish Dot

Use nail polish to make a dot on the top and bottom of the pencil where you would like a student to place his or her thumb (on the bottom) and index finger (on the top). The dots should be about 1" (2.5 cm) above the sharpened end of the pencil. Once the thumb and index finger are in the correct position, demonstrate for the child where the middle finger and remaining fingers should be. The nail polish dots help serve as a reminder of the correct finger placement. For an alternative, place small dot stickers in the correct positions on the pencil.

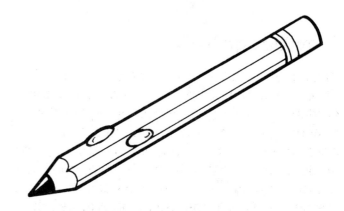

Finger Dots

If a child is holding his or her thumb straight, place a dot of nail polish, paint, or a small sticker on the joint or knuckle of the thumb. This small dot serves as a visual reminder that the thumb should be bent for an efficient pencil grip. Encourage each student to "poke out the dot" when holding a pencil.

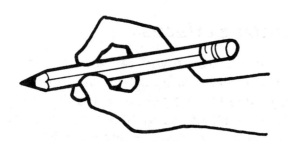

Rubber Band Hold

For a student who is having difficulty holding his or her pencil upright, place a rubber band around the student's wrist. (Be sure that the rubber band is not too tight.) Thread another rubber band through the one on the wrist, and attach it toward the tip of the pencil. The rubber band will help hold the pencil in an upright position.

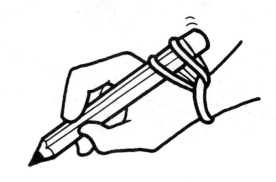

Pencil Grip Activities *(cont.)*

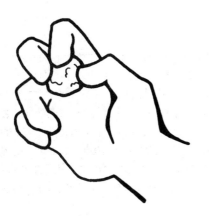

Paper-Ball Hold

For a child having difficulty forming the circle needed for an acceptable pencil grip, have him or her practice holding a paper ball. Wad a piece of paper into a ball. Have the child hold the paper ball with his or her thumb, index finger, and middle finger.

Play Dough Wrap

Wrap play dough around a student's pencil. Then, have him or her use the pencil. If the student is holding the pencil too tightly, the play dough will have changed shape in the area where he or she gripped the pencil. For a student having difficulty in this area, continue to have him or her use the play dough wrap on the pencil. Challenge the student to use the pencil for writing without having the play dough move or change shape.

Writing Surfaces

Provide practice on various types of paper and writing surfaces for a student who presses too firmly while using a pencil. Have the student write on a napkin, sand paper, construction paper, and wax paper. Place the different types of paper on a variety of writing surfaces including: sand paper, napkins, carpet, a pillow, chalkboard, and another child's back. Try having the student write on a sheet of white paper on the carpet. The student will have to adjust how hard he or she presses with the pencil so that a hole will not be poked in the paper. Place the paper on top of a variety of surfaces.

Drawing Activities

Activities especially designed to help students gain control of a pencil (or other writing tool) are provided on pages 185–209. Select pages that are appropriate for your students who need additional practice.

Free Drawing

Once a student begins using a pencil as a writing tool, be sure to allow plenty of time for the student to get used to holding the pencil and manipulating it. A plain sheet of white paper is the best place to start. As the student becomes more skilled at manipulating the pencil, begin to introduce some of the activities on the following pages to help him or her develop better control of the pencil.

Straight Lines

Save cards that are perforated. (These types of cards can be found in magazines, as well as the junk mail you receive.) A student traces the perforated line on the card. The perforated line helps a student keep his or her pencil straight, thus producing a straight line.

Tracing Cards

Draw various types of lines across blank index cards. First draw straight lines, then jagged, and finally curvy. Model how to trace the lines. Then have each student trace the lines, always moving from the left to the right.

Tracing Shapes

Place a piece of plastic, such as a lid to a coffee can, over one of the patterns on pages 178–179. Trace the pattern onto the plastic with a permanent marker. Using a craft knife or scissors, cut out the shape of the pattern. Provide the plastic patterns for your students to practice tracing around. A student uses one hand to hold the pattern in place, and the other hand to hold the pencil. Other objects that students can trace around include: cookie cutters, glasses or cups, various sizes of paper plates, paper clips, buttons, beans, etc. The smaller the object, the more pencil control the student will need.

Teacher Note: A variety of plastic and cardboard stencils can be purchased inexpensively. Provide these stencils and white paper for students to practice tracing shapes.

Drawing Activities *(cont.)*

Walking a Tightrope

Directions: Trace each tightrope line with your finger, then with a pencil. Color the pictures.

Drawing Activities *(cont.)*

Shadows

Directions: Draw a line from each object to its shadow. Color the pictures with crayons.

Drawing Activities *(cont.)*

Matching Mittens

Directions: Draw a line to match each pair of mittens. Color the mittens with crayons. Use the same colors for each pair.

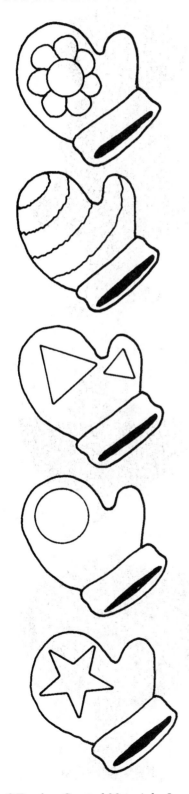

Drawing Activities *(cont.)*

Lost Mittens

Directions: Trace each line with your finger, then with a pencil. Color the pictures.

Drawing Activities *(cont.)*

Going Home

Directions: Trace each line with your finger, then with a pencil. Color the pictures.

Drawing Activities *(cont.)*

Bears and Buttons

Directions: Trace each line with your finger, then with a pencil. Color the pictures.

Drawing Activities *(cont.)*

Where Are the Circles?

Directions: Trace each circle with your finger, then with a pencil. Color the balloons.

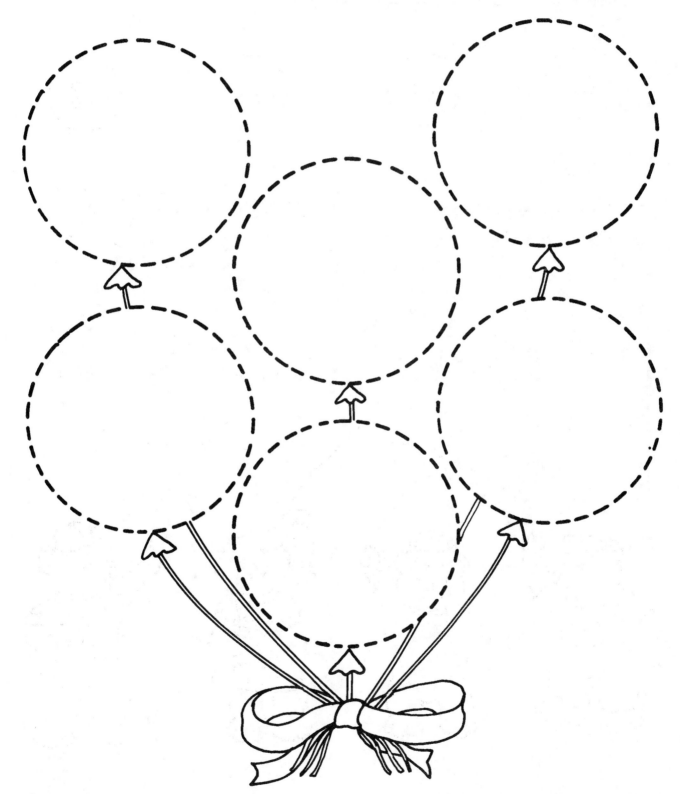

Drawing Activities *(cont.)*

Where Are the Squares?

Directions: Trace each square with your finger, then with a pencil. Color the bus. Draw people in the windows. Add details to the bus.

Drawing Activities *(cont.)*

Where Are the Triangles?

Directions: Trace each triangle with your finger, then with a pencil. Color the pumpkin.

Drawing Activities *(cont.)*

Shape Tracing

Directions: Trace each shape with your finger, then with a pencil. Color the shapes.

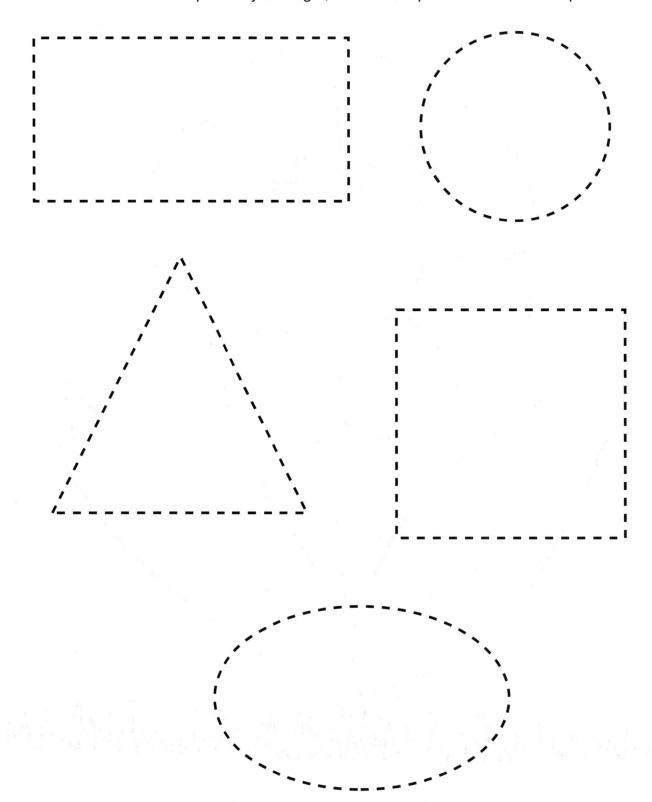

Drawing Activities *(cont.)*

Flower Power

Directions: Trace the line and circle to finish the picture. Color the flower.

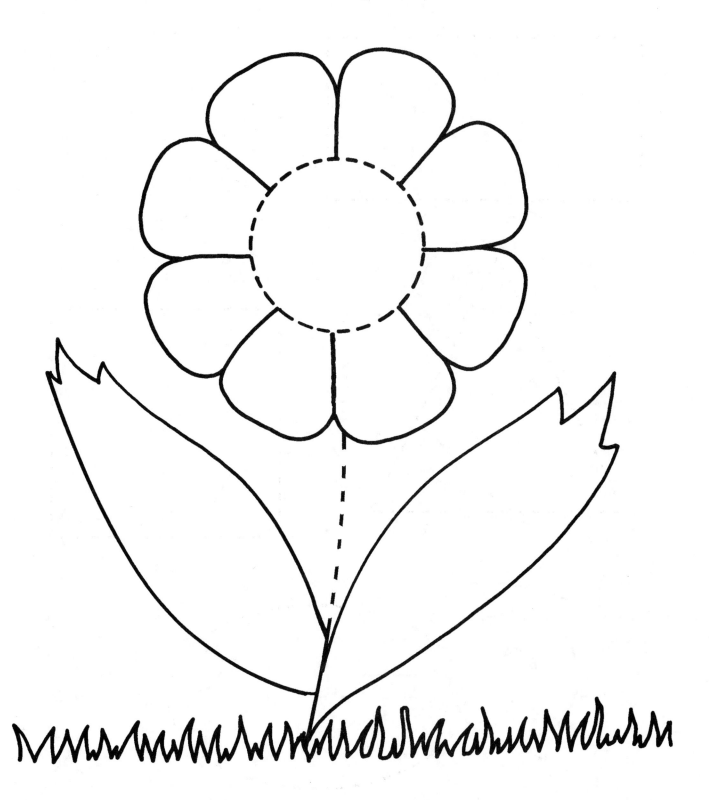

Drawing Activities *(cont.)*

Vroom!

Directions: Trace the lines to finish the pictures. Color the cars.

Drawing Activities *(cont.)*

Match Up

Directions: Draw a line on each shape on the right to make it look like the shape on the left. Color the shapes.

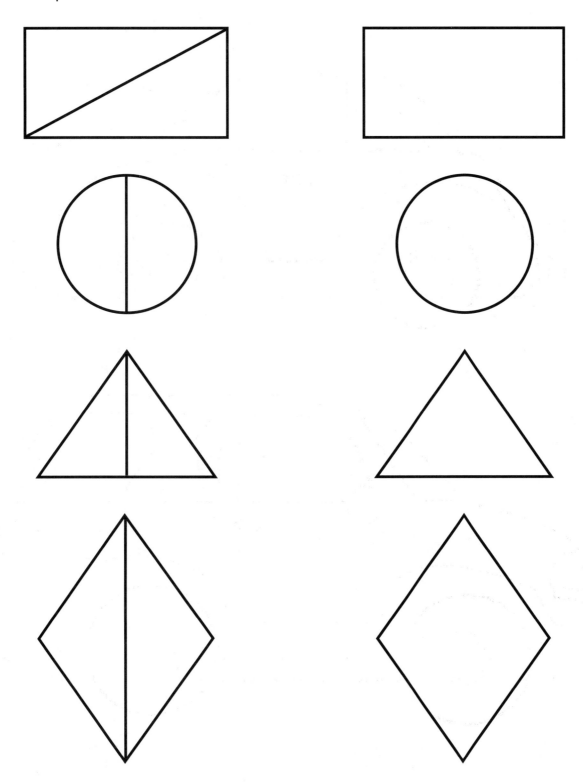

Drawing Activities *(cont.)*

Half and Half

Directions: Complete each shape by drawing the second half to match the first half. Connect the dotted lines on the first shape to see how it's done. Color the shapes.

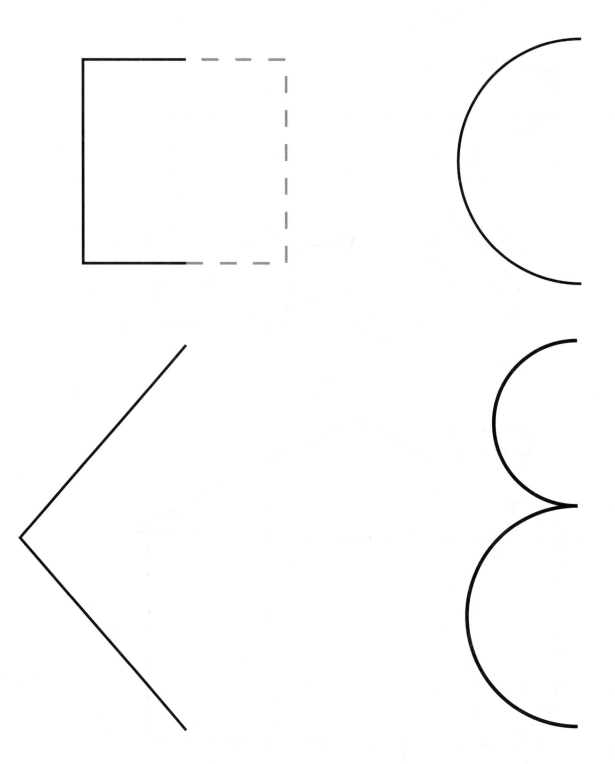

Drawing Activities *(cont.)*

Complete the Pictures

Directions: Complete each picture. Color the dog and the house.

Drawing Activities *(cont.)*

Draw a Fish

Directions: Follow the steps to draw a fish in the blank box. Color your fish.

Drawing Activities *(cont.)*

Draw a Cat

Directions: Follow the steps to draw a big cat. Color your cat.

Drawing Activities *(cont.)*

Catch the Dog

Directions: Help Officer Fritz catch Runaway Dog! Find your way through the maze with a pencil. Color the pictures with a crayon.

Drawing Activities *(cont.)*

Find the Ballerina

Directions: Help the soldier find the ballerina. Find your way through the maze with a pencil. Color the pictures.

Drawing Activities *(cont.)*

Find Your Way Home

Directions: Help Molly find her way home. Find your way through the maze with a pencil. Color the pictures.

Drawing Activities *(cont.)*

Slow and Easy Wins

Directions: Connect the dots from 1–12 to find out who won the race. Color the picture.

Drawing Activities *(cont.)*

Number Bear

Directions: Connect the dots from 1–20 to finish the picture. Color the picture.

206

Drawing Activities *(cont.)*

Surprise

Directions: Connect the dots from 1–20 to finish the picture. Color the picture.

Drawing Activities *(cont.)*

The Mouse Ran up the Clock

Directions: Connect the dots from A to Z. Color the picture.

Drawing Activities *(cont.)*

A Little Cub

Directions: Connect the dots from a to z. Color the picture.

Letter and Number Books

Pages 215–232 provide patterns for students to practice identifying and writing letters and numbers. These pages can be used in a wide variety of ways. For each letter, many different activities can be completed. The alphabet letter pages can be compiled to form an alphabet book. The number pages can be compiled into a number book. Printed on the left side of each page is a letter or number. Choose one of the following activities for students to complete on the left side of the page.

Outline Trace

Have each student trace the outline of the letter or number with one or more of the following: paint, a pencil, marker, colored pencil, glue, colored glue, glitter glue, crayon. For additional practice, have him or her trace the letter more than once with a different medium. For example, the first time the student traces the letter or number using a pencil. The second time, have him or her use a crayon. Finally, the student traces the letter or number with paint and a paintbrush.

Raised Letters

A child squeezes glue on top of a letter or number, following the line. When the glue dries, it will be a raised surface for the student to run his or her fingers on. Add a few drops of food coloring or glitter to the glue for a special treat. Glitter glue is an excellent resource for this activity; it can be purchased, and has a good consistency.

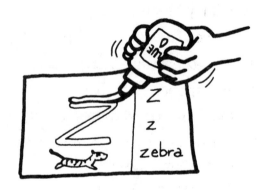

Rainbow-Outline

Have students trace around the shape of the letter or number. A student chooses one color of crayon and traces around the letter or number. Then, he or she chooses another color and traces around the crayon line that was previously drawn. The child selects another color crayon and traces around the most recent outline. Continue this pattern until reaching the edge of the paper.

Letter and Number Books *(cont.)*

Multi-sensory Manipulatives

Provide a variety of materials for students to glue on top of a letter or number outline. You may use accessible objects such as beans, macaroni, or rice, or you may want to use objects that correspond to the featured alphabet letter. Choose from the following objects:

A—Acorns, apple stickers

B—Beans, bird seed, buttons, bow tie pasta, brads, burlap

C—Candy, cotton balls, corn kernels, crayons (broken), cereal, candles, confetti, caps, corks

D—Dots, dough

E—Erasers, egg shells

F—Flour, feathers, felt, fabric, fuzz, fur, flower petals

G—Glitter, granola, glue (colored), gauze

H—Hole punches, heart punches

I—Ink, icing

J—Jelly beans, junk, jewelry, pieces of jump-rope

K—Kidney beans

L—Leaves, licorice, lace, lip gloss, lima beans,

M—Magazine pages, macaroni

N—Newspaper, nuts, noodles, netting

O—Oats, o-shaped cereal, orange ovals (cut outs)

P—Packing peanuts, peanuts, paper curls, pipe cleaners, pasta, popcorn, peas (dried), paper clips

Q—Q-tips®, "quick" sand

R—Rice, raisins, red rectangles, rope

S—Sand, pieces of sponge, salt, sticks, sugar (colored), spaghetti

T—Toothpicks, tube noodles, twigs, tapioca

U—Umbrellas (miniature)

V—Velvet, vanilla pudding, Velcro®

W—White tissue, wiggle eyes, wood chips

X—Cardboard box pieces, floor tile separators (hardware store)

Y—Yellow yarn

Z—Zig zags (ric-rac fabric trim), zippers

Letter and Number Books *(cont.)*

The right side of each page provides printing practice for students. First, have a student trace over the outline of the letters or numbers, then print as many letters or numbers as space allows. The pages may be copied out of this book exactly as they appear, or you may wish to create a whole page for each letter of the alphabet or number. In order to create a whole page, simply cover the portion of the page that you do not want to appear with another sheet of white paper and photocopy. This results in half of the page being printed (as in the book); the other half of the page will be blank. Select one of the following activities for each student to complete on the blank portion of the page.

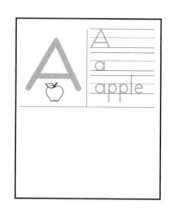

Letter/Number Hunt

Have students search through magazines and newspapers for examples of that letter or number. Students can find letters and numbers in various fonts, sizes, and colors. Encourage them to find several examples of both uppercase and lowercase letters. Then, have each student glue the examples of the featured letter or number on the bottom of his or her page.

Magazine Picture Hunt

Searching through magazines to locate pictures that begin with a particular letter can be a challenging activity. For students who are ready, it is excellent practice in isolating and identifying the first letter in a word. Provide magazines or other printed materials for students to search through to find pictures. Challenge each student to locate three pictures for the letter of the alphabet on which you are currently working. For a student who needs an extra challenge, have him or her search for pictures that end with the letter on which you are working. If you are working on a certain number, have each student locate examples of that number. For example, each student can find four different dogs. After the student has located several examples of the featured letter or number, have him or her glue the examples on the bottom of his or her page.

Letter and Number Books *(cont.)*

Crayon Relief

On the bottom of a student's alphabet or number book page, have him or her use a crayon to write both uppercase and lowercase examples of the letter (or number) being emphasized. The more pressure a student puts on the crayon, the better the crayon relief turns out. He or she paints over the crayon writing with watered-down tempera paint (about half water and half tempera paint) and allows it to dry. The result is a beautiful way for the student to "illustrate" an alphabet letter or number practice.

Pipe Cleaner Shapes

Provide pipe cleaners for each student to make the shape of the letter or number being emphasized. Once the letter has been shaped, assist the student in dipping the letter in glue and gluing it to the bottom of his or her page.

Stamp It

Collect a variety of objects students can use to stamp. Allow students to experiment with the stamps to make the outline of a letter or number. The following materials can be used as stamps: marshmallows, raisins, beans, eraser tips, lids, and golf tees. Try using a variety of materials for "ink" including: tempera paint, watercolors, glue with glitter mixed in it, and glue with sand mixed in it. Then, have each student stamp the featured number or letter on the bottom of his or her page.

Letter and Number Books *(cont.)*

Alphabet and Number Book Covers

My
Alphabet Book

By: _____

My
Number Book

By: _____

Letter and Number Books *(cont.)*

Alphabet Book Pages

Letter and Number Books *(cont.)*

Alphabet Book Pages *(cont.)*

C

c

cow

D

d

dog

Letter and Number Books *(cont.)*

Alphabet Book Pages *(cont.)*

E

E

e

egg

F

F

f

flower

Letter and Number Books (cont.)

Alphabet Book Pages (cont.)

G   G g

       g

       glue

H   H

       h

       hammer

Letter and Number Books *(cont.)*

Alphabet Book Pages *(cont.)*

I

I

i

igloo

J

J

j

jeep

Letter and Number Books *(cont.)*

Alphabet Book Pages *(cont.)*

K

koala

L

lizard

Letter and Number Books *(cont.)*

Alphabet Book Pages *(cont.)*

M M m mitten

N N n net

Letter and Number Books (cont.)

Alphabet Book Pages (cont.)

O o owl

P p pizza

Letter and Number Books *(cont.)*

Alphabet Book Pages *(cont.)*

Q

q

quail

R

r

rake

Letter and Number Books (cont.)

Alphabet Book Pages (cont.)

S

S
s
snail

T

T
t
turtle

Letter and Number Books *(cont.)*

Alphabet Book Pages *(cont.)*

U u

U

u

unicorn

V v

V

v

violin

Letter and Number Books *(cont.)*

Alphabet Book Pages *(cont.)*

W

w

w

web

X

x

x

fox

Letter and Number Books *(cont.)*

Alphabet Book Pages *(cont.)*

Y y

y

yarn

Z z

z

z

zebra

Letter and Number Books *(cont.)*

Number Book Pages

0

O   O   O

|

H

H

H   duck

Letter and Number Books (cont.)

Number Book Pages (cont.)

2

2
2
2
2 cats

3

3
3
3 kites

Letter and Number Books (cont.)

Number Book Pages (cont.)

4

4 dogs

5

5 frogs

Letter and Number Books (cont.)

Number Book Pages (cont.)

6

6

6

6 flowers

7

7

7

7 apples

Letter and Number Books (cont.)

Number Book Pages (cont.)

8

8 books

q

q hearts

Recipes

Play Dough

Cooked Dough

Ingredients:

- 4 cups (950 mL) flour
- 4 cups (950 mL) water
- 2 cups (475 mL) salt
- 2 tablespoons (30 mL) cooking oil
- 1 small container cream of tartar
- food coloring

Directions: Mix and heat until ingredients form a ball. Remove from heat when play dough reaches the correct consistency. Cool and store in a sealed, air-tight container.

No-Cook Dough

Ingredients:

- 2 cups (475 mL) self-rising flour
- 2 tablespoons (30 mL) alum
- 2 tablespoons (30 mL) cooking oil
- 2 tablespoons (30 mL) salt
- 1¼ cups (300 mL) boiling water
- food coloring (optional)

Directions: Mix and knead, adding food coloring if desired. Store the dough in a sealed, air-tight container.

Teacher Note: To make Smelly Play Dough, follow the recipe above and add liquid flavorings for smell.

Goopy Dough

Ingredients:

- 1½ cups (540 mL) flour
- ½ cup (120 mL) salt
- 1 tablespoon (15 mL) alum
- 2 cups (480 mL) boiling water
- 2½ tablespoons (37 mL) cooking oil
- wintergreen scent (optional)
- food coloring (optional)

Directions: Mix and knead, adding food coloring and scent if desired. Store in a sealed, air-tight container.

Recipes *(cont.)*

Play Dough *(cont.)*

No-Fail Dough

Ingredients:

- 1½ cups (360 mL) flour
- ¾ cup (180 mL) salt
- 1½ cups (360 mL) water
- 1½ tablespoons (22 mL) cooking oil
- food coloring (optional)

Directions: Sift dry ingredients. Mix liquids and add coloring if desired. Pour dry ingredients into liquid mixture. Cook over low to moderate heat, stirring constantly, until thickened mixture begins to loosen from sides of the pan. Knead. Cool. Store in a plastic bag or sealed, air-tight container. (This dough does not need refrigeration.)

Powdered Drink Dough

Ingredients:

- 2½ cups (600 mL) flour
- ½ cup (120 mL) salt
- 2 packages unsweetened powdered drink mix
- 3 tablespoons (45 mL) cooking oil
- 2 cups (480 mL) boiling water

Directions: Mix dry ingredients by hand. Add oil and water. Stir quickly. When cooled, mix with hands. Store in a sealed, air-tight container.

Teacher Note: Try a variety of powdered drink mixes for different colors and smells.

Preschool Dough

Ingredients:

- 2 cups (480 mL) flour
- 2 cups (480 mL) water
- 1 tablespoon (15 mL) oil
- 1 cup (240 mL) salt
- 2 teaspoons (10 mL) cream of tartar
- food coloring (optional)

Directions: Mix all ingredients together in a saucepan. Cook and stir until mixture thickens and starts to stick to the pan. Knead out the lumps. Cool completely. Store tightly covered.

Recipes *(cont.)*

Play Dough *(cont.)*

Shampoo Dough

Ingredients:

- ¾ cup (180 mL) flour
- ¼ cup (60 mL) thick shampoo
- ¼ cup (60 mL) white glue

Directions: Mix all ingredients together in a bowl. Knead until smooth. If needed, add more flour to create a workable consistency. Roll and cut into desired shapes. Let dry and paint.

Baker's Clay

Ingredients:

- 4 cups (960 mL) flour
- 1½ cups (360 mL) water
- 1 cup (240 mL) salt

Directions: Mix all ingredients together. Knead for six minutes. Add more flour if the dough is sticky. Form shapes. Bake at 350°F (180°C) for one hour.

Peanut Butter Play Dough

Ingredients:

- 1 cup (240 mL) peanut butter
- 2 tablespoons (45 mL) brown sugar
- 1 tablespoon (15 mL) uncooked oats
- 1 cup (240 mL) corn syrup
- 1½ cups (360 mL) powdered sugar
- 1½ cups (360 mL) powdered milk (dry)

Directions: Mix the ingredients with your hands and add more sugar or powdered milk, as needed. If desired, add more oats for texture.

Teacher Note: This dough is edible; however, check for food allergies before allowing students to eat the dough.

Recipes (cont.)

Play Dough (cont.)

Mashed Potato Candy Dough

Ingredients:

- 1 box powdered sugar
- 2 tablespoons (30 mL) mashed potatoes
- 2 tablespoons (30 mL) melted margarine
- a few drops of milk

Directions: Mix all ingredients together. Add more powdered sugar or milk, as needed.

Homemade Silly Dough

Ingredients:

- 1 cup (240 mL) water (divided)
- ½ cup (120 mL) white glue
- 1 teaspoon (5 mL) Borax®
- food coloring
- corn starch

Directions: Mix ½ cup (120 mL) water, the glue, and the food coloring together. In a separate cup, mix the rest of the water and the Borax®. Combine the two sets of ingredients and knead until the glue forms a putty-like consistency. Add corn starch gradually until it becomes a solid mass. Store in a resealable plastic bag or container.

Coffee-Ground Dough

Ingredients:

- 2 cups (480 mL) coffee grounds
- 1½ cups (360 mL) cornmeal
- ½ cup (120 mL) salt
- water

Directions: Mix coffee grounds, cornmeal, and salt together. Slowly add enough water to make the dough pliable.

Recipes *(cont.)*

Play Dough *(cont.)*

Soap Dough

Ingredients:

- 2 cups (480 mL) soap flakes
- 2 tablespoons (30 mL) water
- food coloring (optional)

Directions: Pour soap flakes into a bowl. Gradually add water until the soap forms a ball when mixed with hands. Add food coloring, if desired. Form shapes and let dry.

Paints

Salt Paint

Ingredients:

- 2 drops of food coloring
- paper plates
- ⅛ cup (30 mL) water
- ½ cup (120 mL) salt
- paintbrush

Directions: Mix starch, water, food coloring, and salt. Use the paint with a paint brush. Keep stirring the mixture while you use it. As the paint dries, it will crystallize.

Tempera Salt Paint

Ingredients:

- 2 tablespoons (30 mL) salt
- 1 tablespoon (15 mL) water
- 1 tablespoon (15 mL) liquid starch
- a few drops of liquid tempera paint

Directions: Mix all ingredients together in a small bowl. This is a roughly-textured paint.

Recipes *(cont.)*

Paints *(cont.)*

Finger Paint—I

Ingredients:

- 3 cups (720 mL) liquid starch
- ½ cup (120 mL) water
- powdered tempera paint (enough to create the shade you want)

Directions: Mix all ingredients. Store in a closed container.

Finger Paint—2

Ingredients:

- 3 cups (720 mL) liquid starch
- 1 cup (240 mL) soap flakes
- ¼ cup (60 mL) water
- powdered tempera paint

Directions: Mix and heat all ingredients (except paint) in a pan. Boil to dissolve. When cool, add tempera paint. Stir. Store in a covered container.

Finger Paint—3

Ingredients:

- 2 cups (480 mL) liquid starch
- 2 cups (480 mL) cold water
- 2 cups (480 mL) soap flakes
- 6 cups (1.5 L) hot water
- powdered tempera paint

Directions: Mix and stir starch and cold water into a paste. Add hot water and cook until thick, stirring constantly. Add soap and tempera paint, stirring until the texture is smooth.

Recipes *(cont.)*

Paints *(cont.)*

Soap Paint

Ingredients:

- 3 cups (720 mL) soap flakes
- ½ cup (120 mL) hot water

Directions: Mix ingredients in a bowl. Whip with an eggbeater until stiff. Do not store this paint—make and use it as needed. (Do not use soap powder since it will not stiffen.)

Sensory Experiences

Bubbles

Ingredients:

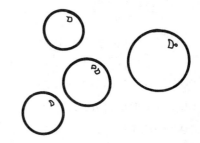

- 2 cups (480 mL) dishwashing liquid
- 6 cups (1.5 L) water
- ¾ cup (180 mL) white corn syrup

Directions: Combine the ingredients, shake in a sealed container, and let settle for four hours. Store in a covered container in the refrigerator. Allow to warm before use.

Teacher Note: Children under four years of age require supervision while using bubbles. This formula is non-toxic, but soap is an eye irritant. Use in the shade. Sunlight weakens the suds.

Oobeleegook

Ingredients:

- cornstarch
- water

Directions: Put cornstarch in a bowl. Add water slowly and let the children mix the ingredients with their hands. The mixture is hard when squeezed, but will run through fingers like liquid.

Recipes *(cont.)*

Sensory Experiences *(cont.)*

Sludge Mud

Ingredients:

- 1 roll of toilet tissue
- 1 cup (240 mL) soap flakes
- 1 tablespoon (15 mL) Borax®
- water

Directions: Rip tissue into small pieces and place in a bowl. Add the rest of the ingredients and mix well. This will create a slippery, slushy, muddy compound (enough for one child).

Creamy Finger Paint

Ingredients:

- shaving or whipping cream
- food coloring

Directions: Place whipping or shaving cream on a cookie sheet or directly on a table for a large play surface. (Whipping cream is best used on a cookie sheet.) Add colors desired by the children. Surprisingly, cleanup is easy.